The Animal Question

The **Animal Question**

Why Nonhuman Animals Deserve Human Rights

Paola Cavalieri
Translated by Catherine Woollard
Revised by the author

OXFORD
UNIVERSITY PRESS

2001

Santiago Canyon College
Library

OXFORD
UNIVERSITY PRESS

Oxford   New York

Athens   Auckland   Bangkok   Bogotá   Buenos Aires   Cape Town
Chennai   Dar es Salaam   Delhi   Florence   Hong Kong   Istanbul   Karachi
Kolkata   Kuala Lumpur   Madrid   Melbourne   Mexico City   Mumbai
Nairobi   Paris   São Paulo   Shanghai   Singapore   Taipei   Tokyo   Toronto   Warsaw

and associated companies in
Berlin   Ibadan

Published by Oxford University Press, Inc.
198 Madison Avenue, New York, New York 10016

An earlier version of this book was published in Italian as
La Questione Animale by Bollati Boringhieri in 1999

Oxford is a registered trademark of Oxford University Press

Library of Congress Cataloging-in-Publication Data
Cavalieri, Paola, 1950–
[Questione animale. English]
The animal question : why nonhuman animals deserve human rights
Paola Cavalieri; translated by Catherine Woollard.
p. cm.
Includes bibliographical references and index.
ISBN 0-19-514380-9
1. Animal rights. 2. Speciesism. I. Title.
HV4708 .C4313   2002
179′.3—dc21   2001036835

1 2 3 4 5 6 7 8 9

Printed in the United States of America
on acid-free paper

Preface

In recent years, nonhuman animals have been at the center of an intense philosophical debate. Many authors have criticized traditional morality, maintaining that the way in which we treat members of species other than our own is ethically indefensible. Taking this shared idea as a starting point, some have provided a reformulation of the moral status of nonhumans based on their own specific normative positions.

My line of reasoning will be different. Instead of proceeding from a particular ethical perspective, I will start from premises that are, as far as possible, shared. I will then attempt to explore what they actually imply. What I shall develop will be, in other words, a dialectical argument.

The aim of the first part of the book is to put the animal question in context. The first chapter focuses on recent cultural changes both in the philosophical and in the scientific domain. In the second, the problem of the structure of the moral community will be explored, and an inclusive criterion will be put forward. I will employ the results thus reached as a framework within which to discuss, in the third chapter, the main defenses of the traditional position.

Once these foundations have been laid, I will confront the fundamental issue: from a moral point of view, how much do nonhuman animals count? The fourth chapter is devoted to a critique of the idea that it is possible to draw a line between our species and other species that creates two distinct moral categories. In the fifth, I will examine some of the recent attempts to reconstruct the moral community so as to avoid any arbitrariness and group loyalty. I will suggest that, although a route can be identified, many problems remain unresolved. In the sixth chapter, finally, after showing that we already have at our disposal a theory that provides an answer to some of these questions, I will claim that this theory cannot be confined to human beings without severe inconsistency. In other words, my conclusion will be that among those entitled to that minimum of equality and equity that allows one to live a life worth living, there are many nonhuman beings whom we currently treat as little more than mere things.

Anyone interested in the topic of our ethical relations with nonhuman animals owes a debt to Peter Singer; in my case this debt has grown through years of collaboration and discussion. I am deeply, and especially, grateful to Harlan B. Miller for his unsparing help and his constructive and often witty criticism. I owe special philosophical debts to Steve F. Sapontzis and to James Rachels, whose moral views taught me even more than is already evident from the text. Sue Donaldson and Will Kymlicka earned my gratitude for their encouragement and for their helpful advice. And, most of all, I thank Franco Salanga, without whose unswerving cooperation and support this book would not exist.

Contents

The Animal Question

Chapter 1

•••

The Cultural Premises

The appearance of new subjects on the social scene is usually accompanied by a questioning of the status quo. And often the process takes place in a number of different areas simultaneously, eroding, so to speak, the cultural paradigm in a roundabout way, and paving the way for a more direct challenge.

In the case of nonhuman animals, the paradigm is both rooted and pervasive. Rooted because it is supported by more than twenty centuries of philosophical tradition aiming at excluding from the ethical domain members of species other than our own. Pervasive because its implications affect many aspects of our lives. But, above all, the paradigm has a vast range of practical consequences. We currently use nonhuman animals as means to our ends. We kill them for food, we use them in our work and entertainment, we employ them as tools in research of all kinds, and it is rare that we pause to ask ourselves whether our behavior is morally justified. Certainly, in theory, we acknowledge the obligation not to cause unnecessary suffering, but our needs are interpreted in such a broad way as to make this constraint negligible. In short, nonhuman animals are at the bottom of a pyramid, at the apex of which we have placed ourselves.

Hierarchical attitudes of this type, of course, are not new. Aristotle thought that slaves were the tools of their owners, and for a long time humans of Caucasian origin theorized their own superiority to members of other races. As in the case of animals, the justification put forward sometimes referred to psychological characteristics, and sometimes, more directly, to a biological aspect, like race membership. Yet the history of what we call moral progress can for the most part be seen as the history of the substitution of hierarchical visions with presumptions in favor of equality.[1] The animal question is therefore part of an ongoing cultural process.

In recent decades, three fields of thought have contributed most to the revival of this process. The first two are philosophical in character, one concerned with the general problem of human equality, and the other with the morality of certain specific practices, in particular abortion and euthanasia. The third sphere is instead scientific, and it involves, essentially if not exclusively, the disciplines that are today grouped together under the label of cognitive sciences. We will consider each of these spheres in turn.

A Problem for Political Philosophy: How to Establish Human Equality

Midway through the 1960s, Richard Wasserstrom, in a piece commissioned by the American Philosophical Association, described as follows the renewed interest in the question of equality:

> This renaissance has been influenced, I believe, by certain events of recent history—notably the horrors of Nazi Germany and the increasingly obvious injustices of racial discrimination in both the United States and Africa.[2]

These elements, to which one could shortly add the ideological pressure of the rising women's liberation movement, undoubtedly played a role in urging political philosophers to deal with a crucial problem: How might one plausibly establish and defend the idea that all human beings are equal? How should a principle of equality capable of constituting a barrier against all forms of discrimination be formulated?

The idea of human equality had, obviously, already been devised in the past. From the doctrine of natural law, passing through Locke, the main constraints on the treatment of human beings had been formulated in terms of equal fundamental rights. But such assertions often remained completely abstract. Locke himself, like other theorists of natural rights, openly sanctioned servitude. Many philosophers of the French Enlightenment did likewise: common among them was the thesis that if equality was nature's first "intention," inequality was natural in the secondary sense of being necessary for the order and well-being of society. Even Montesquieu, who did so much to undermine the traditional justifications of slavery, maintained that such a practice, although contrary to natural law, had, at least in some "tropical countries," a function to perform.[3] It is no surprise then that the Declaration of Independence of the United States asserted that all men [sic] were created equal at a time when slavery flourished in the southern states. Declarations of principle were never substantially matched by a consistent plan of political implementation.

When contemporary philosophers set to work, however, what they had behind them was not so much a period of fluctuations and inconsistencies but rather the long post-Enlightenment phase of a rejection of equality even at the theoretical level. It was having to start afresh that gave their effort its depth. The most pressing problem they had to confront was that of discrimination based on sex or race. A long tradition tended to attribute factual inferiority to women and blacks—lower intelligence, inferior rationality, a lower degree of autonomy—and to use this as the basis for justification of differential treatment. How might this attitude be opposed?

The simplest rejoinder obviously lay in trying to demonstrate that such "inferiority" does not in fact exist, and, in particular, that there are no differences between the sexes and the races as groups. We will see later on that this is a path that was followed by some authors and that is still deemed plausible. It has, however, a fundamental defect: if moral equality is made dependent on actual empirical equality, if it were to be shown that the members of the various human groups are indeed different, we should have to give up treating them as equals. Would we be prepared to accept racial discrimination if it were demonstrated, by overwhelming evidence, that certain races show on the whole a lower level of, for example, abstract reasoning? Certainly not.

What is one to think of such a reaction? It could be purely unreflective, the fruit of prejudices that should be modified. Or, on the contrary, it could be the sign of a true theoretical dissatisfaction. By the way, it is important to notice that the adoption of the criterion of empirical equality, with its implicit acceptance of a hierarchy among the faculties, would not merely imply the risk of a reversion to possible forms of racism. Other types of discrimination opposed by egalitarians would also regain plausibility. Why not classify (as far as it is possible) individual human beings directly on the basis of intelligence? Why not divide social roles and opportunities into separate layers, differently accessible according to cognitive skill?

Confronted with these options, philosophers, convinced that the presumption in favor of equality is not the fruit of mistaken prejudices (and they are the majority), opted for a second alternative. In short, their argument can be summarized as follows: Let's admit what cannot be denied, that is, that human beings are individually different in terms of physical characteristics, ranging from beauty to strength, and intellectual characteristics, ranging from intelligence to will and creativity. We might push this even further and not fear the remote but not impossible eventuality of measurable differences between groups. The problem is that none of this is significant. What matters is that human beings are endowed with conscious interests, and that some of these interests are essential if one is to live a decent life. The satisfaction of our interests is important for each one of us, regardless of race, sex, or intelligence. That I am not white has nothing to do with my interest in freedom. Analogously, that I am not an acclaimed scientist but simply a used car dealer, doesn't impinge in any way on my interest in not suffering. The fundamental interests of each one count, and they should be granted equal consideration regardless of the other characteristics that each may possess.[4] The principle of equality can thus be translated into the principle of equal consideration of interests.

What follows from this thesis? First, the idea of equality loses its trivially descriptive character. To say that human beings are equal no longer means professing that they resemble each other in everything—that they have the same type of sensitivity, the same level of intelligence, and so on. To assert human equality means, rather, acknowledging: (a) that human beings share a basic characteristic, the possession of conscious interests, that makes them proper objects of moral consideration; and (b) that these interests—in particular, the fundamental ones—should be granted equal consideration. It is to this partial recasting of equality in prescriptive terms—to the idea that, apart from the possession of the basic characteristic, equality does not refer to how beings are but to how they should be treated—that we owe the prohibition not only of any kind of group discrimination but also of any reversion to hierarchies based on forms of perfectionism.

With a new consequence, however. The confinement of equality to members of our species has always hinged on high-sounding claims about our rationality and moral capacity. But if the defense of a principle of equality that may include the least among human beings and does not differentiate between the interests of the cultured and the underprivileged, the sane and the mentally ill, or the "civilized" and the "primitive" leads to abandoning such references in order to work on a much more accessible level—where prominence is given to such aspects as the capacity to feel pleasure and pain, to pursue one's goals, and to enjoy one's life—such confinement of equality loses its plausibility. In other words, the new conception pushes against the historical bias in favor of the intellectual that has so long characterized Western philosophy, and it opens the door to the idea that equality cannot go on being solely an internal affair of the species *Homo sapiens*.

As a result of the tradition in which they had been educated and of the fact that their specific problem was that of overcoming the barriers between human beings, the authors working on this question did not fully perceive this turn. They kept maintaining that the sphere of application of the principle they were formulating could plausibly exclude all nonhuman beings. Nevertheless, the very logic of their solutions makes such an exclusion impossible.

Bioethical Dilemmas: Who Is Human?

In their attempt to defend principles that can establish criteria for just conduct, moral philosophers have always examined specific ethical questions: think of Hume's interest in suicide, or Bentham's interest in the problem of punishment. This tradition was suddenly interrupted early in the twentieth century when the positivist school called into question the efficacy of moral reasoning, claiming that the main function of moral terms is not to ascertain truth or falsity but to express emotions. Starting from this idea—and in connection with the linguistic turn that was affecting a number of disciplines—normative ethics was newly contrasted with metaethics, that is, with the second-order reflection focusing on the analysis of moral language. At the same time she acknowledged the theoretical merits of metaethical discourse, Mary Warnock acutely observed that if one bears in mind that the object of morality is not so much the categories we use to describe reality but rather our impact on the world, then it is no surprise that ethics as a discipline underwent a gradual process of trivialization.[5] It was largely as a reaction to the uncommitted attitude that characterized metaethics that, at the beginning of the 1970s, applied ethics was (re)born. Prompted by the demands for "relevance" that came from different social spheres, many moral philosophers started again to defend the idea that argument does have an important role to play in ethics, and they began to apply to a growing number of specific moral dilemmas the theoretical tools produced by linguistic analysis. It is to this encounter between the legacy of the analytic approach and the rediscovered interest in concrete ethical problems that we owe the questioning of many traditional assumptions.

In this process, an important role was soon assumed by bioethics, as the branch of ethics concerned with the moral problems raised by the medical and biological sciences has come to be called. The rapid and continuous growth of our power over life-and-death circumstances inevitably gives rise to new dilemmas, or makes the old ones more pressing. Some questions have to do with behavior: Is it acceptable to offer one's body for surrogate motherhood? Should we permit the creation of a market in organs for transplants? Is genetic screening permissible? When cases of this kind are involved, it is often a matter of stretching the boundaries of traditional ethics, extending or reviewing judgments referring to similar cases. Other questions raise problems concerning the status of the beings affected: What is the value of the life of a human fetus? Does an individual in an irreversible coma have a right to continued existence? Are embryos a kind of entity on which one can experiment? Questions such as these lead one to put to the test, and to challenge, criteria of moral considerability that were taken for granted in the past.

"Life is an irreducible value. Therefore, the value of a particular life, over and above the value of life itself, may not be taken into account."[6] This sentence embodies the kernel of the view which, until recently, was one of the moral ideas most universally accepted in the biomedical field, one which still plays a role both in the opposition to abortion and in the deep-seated resistance of many to euthanasia.

According to this view, better known as the sanctity-of-life doctrine, all lives have equal, absolute value, irrespective of their quality or their kind. Accordingly, it doesn't make sense to ask the questions I mentioned—the life of the embryo, of the fetus, and of the irreversibly comatose count for exactly the same as any other life.

The phrase "sanctity of life" is ambiguous, however. Of what life are we speaking? Obviously not of life in all its forms, including vegetal ones. Of animal life in general, then? Were it so, we would live in a society of vegetarians. Since this is not the case, it is evident that the phrase refers only to human life. A more accurate phrase would thus be "sanctity-of-human-life" doctrine.[7] The lives that are attributed equal, absolute value are the lives of members of the species *Homo sapiens*. Once translated in terms of medical practice, the principle of the sanctity of life requires that the existence of every single human being be prolonged at (almost) any cost.[8]

What lies at the basis of the equal and absolute value of human lives? At first sight, the use of the term "sanctity" seems to have religious overtones. In fact, the doctrine is primarily rooted in a religious context, in particular in God's equal and supreme interest in every human creature. Those who speak of the sanctity of human life today, however, do not always have in mind religious justifications. One could say that what prevails is a secular version of the doctrine, defended both by lay authors and by religious authors who want to appeal to a heterogeneous public. But the problem is this: once it has been stripped of all theological support, is the sanctity-of-life doctrine still defensible? In the course of recent discussions in bioethics, many philosophers have replied that it is not.

To understand their reasons, consider a concrete case: the story of Tony Bland. In 1989, Tony Bland, a young English football fan, was crushed by a crowd pressing to get into a football match. The interruption of breathing due to the compression of his lungs deprived his brain of oxygen for too long and destroyed his cortex, causing the loss of all cognitive functions. Tony Bland was thus reduced to a persistent vegetative state, according to the expression used by the judge who worked on the case. Convinced that there was no chance of recovery, his parents asked—with the agreement of doctors—that their son be deprived of artificial sustenance. In order to avoid the risk of being charged, the director of the hospital to which Tony Bland was admitted requested the authorization of the Family Division of the High Court. The judge entrusted with guarding Tony Bland's interests objected, however, maintaining that the parents' proposal would amount to murder.[9]

What is one to say about this position? From a certain perspective, if murder is the killing of a human being, it cannot be denied that the interruption of artificial sustenance in a case such as that of Tony Bland falls under this description. Tony Bland is certainly human, insofar as he is the son of human parents, and thus the carrier of a human genotype. But is this the sense one can appeal to in order to defend the idea of the sanctity of life? The answer seems to be no. Usually, when we say of a being that it is human, we are assuming an endowment of certain special characteristics, such as self-consciousness, rationality, self-control, sense of time, communicative ability, and the ability to relate to others—that is, the attributes that have been defined "indicators of humanhood."[10] This is the evaluative, or philosophical, sense of "human being"—a sense for which many prefer to use the term "person," as contrasted with the biological notion of "member of the species *Homo sapiens*."

Some authors maintain that whatever value human life might have must rest upon human personhood rather than mere species membership. Even though the concept of person is a complex one (and one to which we will have to return), it is important to underline here that the distinction between "human being" and "person" captures an important point. Our life is the sum of all that counts for us—our well-being, our projects, our activities, and our relationships—and all that counts for us is made possible by the possession of certain capacities. Without these capacities, we would have different interests, and without one capacity in particular, consciousness, we would not have any interests. In a key essay on euthanasia, James Rachels clarified this point well.[11] Beings lacking consciousness, he has claimed, while *biologically* alive—that is, endowed with vital processes and metabolic functioning—lack that which really counts morally, namely, a *biographical* life. They do not have character, history, relationships, or well-being: nothing that happens to them can affect them positively or negatively. If, therefore, it is to the philosophical sense of the notion of human being that the defenders of the sanctity-of-life doctrine refer, then the claim that killing an individual in a persistent vegetative state means killing a human being is patently false.

An echo of this philosophical argument can be found in the effective conclusion of the Bland case. The highest court in the British judicial system, the House of Lords, confirmed the line held by the tribunals that preceded it and granted authorization for the withdrawal of artificial feeding, stating, among other things, that "it is not in the interest of an insentient patient to continue the life-supporting care and treatment."[12] It emerges clearly from this judgment that since the biographical life of Tony Bland came to an end on the day his brain did, the preservation of his merely biological life no longer had any meaning. The same can be said of any irreversibly comatose: none of these human beings is endowed with—picking at random from the list of indicators of humanhood—self-control, a sense of time, or the capacity for interaction with others. To return to the thesis mentioned above, none of these human beings is a person.

The distinction between "human being" and "person" also plays an important role in the debate on the morality of abortion. Brought to the forefront again, not only by the feminist movement but also by the refinement of techniques of prenatal diagnosis of congenital diseases, the problem of abortion is for the most part, although not completely,[13] the problem of the value of the life of the fetus. According to some advocates of the sanctity-of-life doctrine, abortion is a form of murder because the fetus is a person. But if it is true that the term "person" refers to the philosophical sense of "human being" and thus to the possession of characteristics such as self-consciousness or rationality, it is clear that this claim is not plausible. Up to a certain point in gestation, the fetus has no consciousness at all. Subsequently, with the development of the central nervous system, a form of consciousness appears, which, however, even at the moment of birth, is a long way from including the features considered essential to the attribution of personhood. Like the comatose, then, the fetus lacks the cluster of characteristics that lies at the basis of the philosophical sense of "human being." True, unlike the comatose, the fetus has the potential to become a person; but the argument from potentiality, even supposing that it is sound (and this is quite controversial) doesn't change the essential aspect, namely, the possibility of an actual disjunction between being a member of the species *Homo sapiens* and possessing the characteristics considered typically human.

Deeply engrained moral doctrines do not lose their hold overnight. Faced with the impossibility of founding the absolute value of the life of all human beings, and human beings alone, on morally significant characteristics that some of them in fact do not possess, some philosophers chose to defend the attribution of a particular moral value to the merely biological sense of human being. Whether this move is possible is something we will discuss in detail in one of the following chapters. For now, it suffices to point out that it was just the overlapping of the evaluative and the biological sense of human being that made it possible to attribute a particular moral weight to the possession of a genotype characteristic of *Homo sapiens,* thanks to the unjustified extension to all members of the species—including those lacking self-consciousness, rationality, and the like—of the special value connected to the philosophical sense of the notion. The elimination of the ambiguity present in the concept of human being has now precluded such a move, suggesting that it is possible to meet the descriptive criterion for being human without meeting the evaluative criterion, and vice versa. In other words, the bioethical discussion of borderline cases like the fetus and the irreversibly comatose opened the way to the eventuality that mere membership in our species may not necessarily entitle one to the protection guaranteed by the sanctity-of-life doctrine; and that, inversely, the possession of the favored characteristics may render a member of a species other than *Homo sapiens* a plausible candidate for such protection.

After Behaviorism, or How Animal Minds Started to Exist Again

The debate examined at the beginning of this chapter is evidence of the philosophical tendency that characterizes contemporary thought on equality. Nevertheless, as I have already mentioned, it is possible to opt for a different alternative, that is, for the attempt to provide the idea of equality with a purely factual basis. In spite of the risks that the possible discovery of actual empirical inequalities involves, this was one of the routes taken when the theoretical work accompanying the United Nations Declarations on Human Rights was undertaken. If one analyzes the composition of the committees that drafted the two "Statements on Race" of 1950 and 1951, one discovers that all the authors had a scientific background. "With respect to most, if not all, measurable characters," the final document summarizes, "the differences among individuals belonging to the same race are greater than the differences that occur between the observed averages for two or more races."[14]

The recourse to science when discussing normative questions is naturally problematic, insofar as it raises the controversial question of the relation between *is* and *ought*. Nonetheless, there is a weak and relatively uncontroversial sense in which matters of fact can influence values: that according to which new facts, or changes in the way of presenting old ones, can undermine rooted beliefs, allowing one to look at problems in a different way. In a sense, this is what happened with the work of the United Nations experts. After decades of Social Darwinism and theses on the inferiority of some peoples, the assertion that our species is not constituted of different stages of a teleological development but rather is simply composed of population groups that differ from each other according to the frequency of one or more genes arrived like a breath of fresh air.

Something analogous happened in the case of nonhuman animals. It is likely that the deep change in the scientific approach to the animal mind that began in the 1970s has yet to bear all its fruit. However, both epistemologically and from the point of view of the themes of research, it is already like being in a different world. It is worth briefly reconsidering, therefore, the steps in an intellectual shift that—by providing a radically new representation of nonhumans—paved the way for the questioning of their position in the moral community.

Although nearly a century had passed since Darwin advanced his ideas about the continuity between humans and nonhumans, at the end of the 1950s the prevailing vision was still dichotomous. The research scene, in particular in psychology, was dominated by behaviorism. Born in connection with the tenets of logical positivism, from which it derived the aspiration to establish an experimental and quantitative methodology, behaviorism opposed the Cartesian concept of the mind. Its target was the so-called "ghost in the machine." According to the intentions of its founder, J. B. Watson, behaviorism was to take psychology back to the realm of the hard sciences, replacing consciousness with observable behavior, and excluding the use of all terms that couldn't be defined on the basis of detectable relations between stimuli and responses.

In theory, behaviorism maintained that mentalistic explanations were as inappropriate for humans as for nonhumans, and it used the latter as a model for the former. In practice, though, its effects made themselves felt above all in the approach to animals, who, unlike humans, had no protection from powerful opposing theories. Almost unnoticed, the idea of the undemonstrability of the existence of the animal mind transmuted into the assertion of its nonexistence.

It is not difficult to imagine what this meant, particularly in laboratories. What counts in suffering is its phenomenal aspect—the way in which the subject experiences it. But this problem doesn't exist if one speaks of behavioral dispositions. If it is possible to describe an organism in behavioral terms alone, what is omitted is just the mode of description that is required for ethical concern—the one linked to the experiencing subject.[15] In this light, the suspicion arises that part of the attraction of behaviorism might lie in the moral advantages that the deproblematization of the treatment of animals allowed. In any case, the paradoxical result was that the concrete implications for nonhumans of an approach born out of anti-Cartesianism ended up by coinciding with those of the French philosopher's theory. In both cases, animals came to be seen, and treated, as simple automata.

However, the dichotomous approach had other roots too. "Morgan's appeal to simplicity and rejection of anthropomorphism would seem, from a modern perspective, to have made the development of a scientific behaviorism inevitable."[16] This excerpt taken from an everyday manual of psychology from thirty years ago shows, in its concision, the strict links existing between behaviorism and two norms that have for a long time contributed to maintaining the distinction between the human and nonhuman mind. The first is Morgan's Canon, which dictates that no animal behavior may be interpreted at a higher level when it can be interpreted at a lower one. The second is the interdiction of "anthropomorphism," which revolves around the idea that any interpretation of animal behavior that makes reference to human behavior should be censured from a scientific point of view, insofar as it tends to attribute to nonhumans more than their due.

Today, Morgan's Canon has to a large extent lost its previous role. In the hands of behaviorist scientists, it used to be a criterion of parsimony, similar to the famous Occam's razor, which prohibits the unnecessary multiplication of entities; and, according to the dominant interpretation, parsimony was violated by any attribution of mental activity to nonhuman animals. This is not, however, the only possible reading. Just as a criterion of parsimony, in fact, the canon can lead in a direction contrary to that desired by the behaviorists who, obsessed by the rejection of any mentalistic explanation, often needed to have recourse to theories with lesser explanatory power. In other words, from many sides it has been underlined that a criterion of parsimony can favor a simple interpretation at a higher level rather than a complicated explanation at a lower level. Imagine that an animal exhibits a highly versatile behavior, capable of adapting itself to varied and unexpected circumstances. On the basis of the behaviorist interpretation of the canon, we would find here a behavioral repertoire consisting of an extremely complex series of subprocedures started by specific stimuli. However, it is plausible to maintain that, in such a case, the appeal to a certain degree of rationality, capable of setting out a strategy and of modifying it with respect to a given number of changes, represents a definitely simpler and more elegant solution.

Not even the concept of "anthropomorphism" remained immune to criticism. First, the charge of anthropomorphism appears indeed to be question-begging. If, in fact, the problem in question is to verify whether humans and nonhumans share mental properties, one cannot assume a priori that it is unreasonable and unscientific to attribute human mental properties to animals. Furthermore, why lay such a heavy stress on possible disanalogies? We are human, but we are also primates and mammals. From this perspective, some authors have suggested that the incorrect approach is not anthropomorphism but rather that form of anthropocentrism that, afraid of any parallel between us and the other animals, arbitrarily removes our species from the evolutionary mainstream of life.[17] As for the methodological component of the tendency to "anthropomorphize"—which concerns the possibility of drawing on human phenomenology to explain the attitudes and experiences of members of other species—it may be said to have been reappraised and to have recently come to be seen as a useful scientific tool.[18]

Similar shifts in perspective, once inconceivable, have been made possible by the decline of the behaviorist approach. The decline began to be apparent in the 1960s, and a decade later behaviorism had died out in most of the intellectual world. To what was the change due? Although a number of different factors were relevant, without doubt an important role was played by the gradual affirmation of the idea that mechanistic and mentalistic explanations are not incompatible. More specifically, the thesis that emerged was that as it is often appropriate to explain the working of a computer in terms of its program, so it is possible to explain human behavior through reference to mental states. But the compatibility of mentalism and mechanism can be defended at a much more abstract level.

An argument to this effect has been advanced by James Rachels. Suppose that a child is severely punished by her parents every time she tells a lie. As a consequence of this, the child develops a sort of repugnance for lying. Once grown up, the woman never lies, even in situations in which to do so would not be serious, or would even be useful. In such a case, it seems altogether plausible to maintain that her behavior is as much the result of conditioning as the result of her desires. Indeed, it could be said that not only is the mechanistic element compatible with the mentalistic element but that it actually explains it: the woman chooses not to lie precisely because she has been conditioned not to do so. Obviously, this doesn't exclude the possibility of avoiding mentalistic explanations through recourse to specific, general philosophical views about their eliminability. However, to maintain, for external reasons, that scientific psychology has to give up mentalistic terms is something very different from asserting that mentalistic and mechanistic explanations cannot coexist due to their very nature. And while the former assertion may or may not be correct, the latter is definitely incorrect.[19]

In the light of such a general argument, one could ask why, historically, it was just the idea of comparing mentalistic language to the "states" of a computer program that opened a breach in the behaviorist paradigm. And the explanation is simple: because such a parallel can introduce the mind without necessarily introducing consciousness. The computer elaborates information in a complex manner without the intervention of any form of consciousness. From this viewpoint, the birth of the new discipline of cognitive psychology does not mark in itself such a radical break with the past.

Not surprisingly, all this involves the reappearance of the phenomenon of divergent application we have already met with in the case of behaviorism. When what is in question is the human mind, the persistence of mistrust about notions suggesting forms of consciousness is not of much consequence, because of the absolute prevalence of theories that do not dispute in any way the fact that we are conscious. When it comes to nonhumans, on the other hand, such a caution might well turn the attribution of mental states into a Pyrrhic victory. Certainly, if one cannot deny that the social lives of many animals are complex, as an ever growing number of researchers suggest, and if there are no good theoretical reasons to avoid speaking of mental states, the cognitive approach cannot but be extended to the members of other species. And, albeit gradually, this is what happened. But of what consequence might the presence of an unconscious mind be? As regards treatment, moral concern is as out of place for a computer as for an automaton.

Other factors will have to intervene for an effective change to take place. Among them, a prominent role is no doubt to be granted to the publication, in 1974, of "What Is It Like to Be a Bat?" In this now celebrated article, Thomas Nagel not only takes it as a given that many nonhuman animals have experiences, but he also makes use of this starting point to develop his refutation of two cornerstones of behaviorism: the idea that it is possible to eliminate the subjective element from the analysis of the mind, and the idea that the difficulty of understanding the experiences of other minds invalidates the claim that they have experiences.[20] In the course of the debate that followed the publication of this article, many authors engaged in the attempt to formulate a theory of mind that would firmly root psychic phenomena in the natural world. While some remained skeptical with regard to animal consciousness, others confirmed and developed the nondichotomous approach defended by Nagel. Among these was John Searle, who, after claiming that consciousness is a biological process occurring in the brain and is as much a part of the biological natural history of animals as are mitosis or growth, thus summarizes the new perspective:

> Descartes together with the British empiricists and right up through the Positivists and the Behaviorists of the twentieth century have given us the impression that the question: "How do you know?" asks the fundamental question . . Against this tradition, I want to say that epistemology is of relatively little interest in philosophy and daily life. . . . Another way to put this is to say that it doesn't matter really *how* I know whether my dog is conscious, or even *whether* or not I do "know" that he is conscious. The fact is, he is conscious and epistemology in this area has to *start* with this fact.[21]

It happens sometimes that the developments in philosophical reflection have difficulty in spreading beyond the confines of the academic discipline. In spite of the transformations in progress, students of animal behavior, even of a cognitivist bent, for a long time stuck to the idea that the employment of terms like belief, desire, or consciousness could represent a return to the feared Cartesian conception of the mind, and they continued, accordingly, to mistrust it. However, there were exceptions.

Having been for so long—and with so little justification—kept in the background, the Darwinist idea of a mental continuity between humans and nonhumans reemerged, thanks to Donald Griffin. From the 1970s on, the authoritative Harvard-based zoologist published a series of volumes that, as well as including an impressive mass of documentary material, theoretically defended the possibility of attributing conscious thought to animals. Griffin championed, among other things, the birth of a new discipline, cognitive ethology, that would always "keep an open mind" about such a possibility.[22]

It was a good prophecy. The tradition, in the past primarily European, of fieldwork came to be gradually taken up again and revitalized in the Anglo-American arena. With a difference, however. For if the founding fathers of the discipline, such as Tinbergen and Lorenz, while not denying the existence of subjective states in animals, shared with methodological behaviorism the idea that subjectivity cannot be the subject of scientific study, many contemporary ethologists do not hesitate to introduce into their studies reference to animal consciousness. This indicates not only a return to the logical implications of evolutionary theory but also a partial recovery of so-called "folk psychology." After all, it is difficult for anyone who normally has anything to do with an animal to believe that they really have in front of them a being lacking consciousness. It was only to be expected that, sooner or later, there would be a revival of common sense. Griffin is one of the intellectual figures to whom credit for this revival should be ascribed.

Another is without doubt Jane Goodall. At the beginning of the 1960s, during what was still the behaviorist era, Goodall spent a long period alone in the tropical forest of Gombe tracking and studying chimpanzees. Perhaps because she was foreign to the official scientific world, the young researcher had no qualms about using such terms as "childhood," "adolescence," "motivation," and "mood" in the reports of her field observations, and even went so far as to attribute individual personalities to the different chimpanzees. At first, this obviously created a scandal and stirred up the well-known charges of anthropomorphism and violation of scientific objectivity. Gradually, however, the publication of a number of rigorously academic works and the impressive success met with among the public at large prevailed over this opposition, turning Jane Goodall into one of the most important figures in contemporary ethology.

If one were asked to name Goodall's main contribution, the first response would probably make reference to her scientific achievements. Her investigations offered the first detailed reconstruction of the individual and social life of chimpanzees, while at the same time helping to discredit many commonplaces about human uniqueness, starting with the idea that we are the only ones to shape and use tools.[23] There is, however, another aspect that is as important, one that refers not to the results but to the method of research. That primatology has become for animals something similar to what anthropology is for human beings—a theoretical bridge allowing those who are different to get closer—is largely due to the method used by Goodall, which is patently nearer to the subject-subject approach of the social sciences than to the subject-object approach of the natural sciences.[24] Inserting itself within a process already in motion, this change of approach made it easier for an entire generation of ethologists to attribute to nonhuman animals a growing number of complex behavioral traits,[25] ranging from intentional teaching to planning of future activity to sophisticated forms of social cooperation.

Of course, all this did not happen without opposition and criticism. Nothing equaled, however, the reaction elicited by a later, important discovery that came not from the ethological sphere but from the more cautious and conservative discipline of cognitive psychology. At least from Descartes on, linguistic ability has been considered by philosophers the human prerogative par excellence, because of the sophisticated set of cognitive patterns it presupposes. For his part, Darwin believed instead that human language was merely the natural extension of a primitive system of signals similar to those used by other animals.[26] But how can one test such an idea?

Faced with this question, some American researchers worked on the hypothesis that our closest evolutionary relatives might be endowed with a prelinguistic capacity. Verbal language is a form of symbolic communication requiring utterance of particular sounds. As the vocal system of nonhabitual bipeds is, for physical reasons, not capable of producing consonants, the essential problem lay in overcoming this limitation. After a series of failed attempts, this happened through recourse to a gesture-based language. Thanks to the American Sign Language, authors such as Allen and Beatrice Gardner, Roger Fouts,

Francine Patterson, and others claimed that they had finally managed to teach a human language to nonhuman beings—chimpanzees and gorillas.

Immediately, various linguists, Noam Chomsky among them, cast doubts on this claim, lining up in defense of neo-Cartesian theses. But psychologists in the discipline that is now called interspecific communication responded to the criticisms, proving their results with new research and increasingly rigorous tests. Recent data do not allow for any doubts about the fact that nonhuman great apes can develop a vocabulary of hundreds of signs with independent symbol status, and can combine them in a way that meets the fundamental criteria for being recognized as grammatical. On a less abstract level, furthermore, the reports show how individuals growing up in a family environment, just like children, currently employ language for manipulative purposes, start dialogues, and express their own preferences, fears, and emotions.[27]

A further confirmation of the presence of prelinguistic capacity in nonhuman animals comes from studies of intelligent beings evolutionarily distant from us, such as dolphins. Obviously, in such a case it is much easier to observe the passive side of linguistic ability, that is, comprehension as opposed to production. Some bottle-nosed dolphins in captivity have been instructed in artificial languages whose words (comprising substantives, verbs, and qualifiers) consist of computer-generated sounds or video images of the instructor's gestures. According to the reports of the researchers, in short order the dolphins learned to successfully carry out around two thousand commands represented by strings of words, revealing that they can grasp both the semantic and the syntactic aspect.[28] If one thinks of how alien the visual-terrestrial cognitive human environment can be for beings whose natural environment is acoustic-aquatic, and how difficult are the living conditions of so-called marine laboratories, one can realize the real level of these results. Other evidence came from unexpected areas: parrots, for example, have recently demonstrated that they know how to use expressions like "I'm sorry" (after an error in the test) or "wanna go back" (before a visit to the vet), thus exhibiting a use of language capable of going far beyond the purely phonetic imitation traditionally attributed to them.[29]

But the actual teaching of a language to nonhuman animals is not the only way in which the Darwinian thesis can be put to the test. Although with less public recognition, some authors have undertaken the attempt to directly identify a continuity in the relevant cognitive patterns. Since in this case the fundamental methodological question How is it possible to discern the potential for linguistic communication in individuals without a spoken language? is shared with investigations into language learning in children, a theoretical collaboration once difficult to imagine was established between developmental psychologists and comparative psychologists. Research focused on three signs of potential linguistic ability: imitative pretence, intentional deception, and that communication of nonnatural meaning which, according to H. P. Grice, characterizes intentional human communication.[30]

The idea that imitative pretence can in some way forebode language traces back to Bateson's analysis of metacommunication in nonverbal beings. Bateson suggests that play is the typical situation in which a being can simulate its activities and render evident to others the fact of simulation. Of course, social play is, to varying degrees of complexity, widely diffused among nonhuman animals.[31] The second element, intentional deception, is accompanied by the capacity for dual description: in order to deceive one has to be able to distinguish between reality and mental representation, so as to see events from the perspective of the interlocutor, and to attempt to cause mental representations that do not correspond to reality. In animals, deliberate deception has been verified in a number of contexts, which vary from competition for sex or food to the relationship between predator and prey, which can be the source of real strategies.[32]

The attribution of both imitative pretence and intentional deception is in clear contrast to the widespread interpretation of animal behavior that Griffin defined as the "groans of pain view,"[33] because it sees the signals of nonhuman animals as the direct result of internal physiological states—something similar, indeed, to our groans. The degree to which this interpretation is challenged today is further demonstrated by reflection on the last aspect we cited—that is, on the communication of nonnatural meaning. Grice's theory of nonnatural meaning implies that in producing utterances, a communicator presumes that others recognize the communicator's own intention that they do or believe something as a result of the utterance. It thus involves an apparently quite convoluted process, which seems to require, in addition to the presence of metarepresentations, the actual possession of a verbal language. But, as authors such as the Spanish psychologist Juan Carlos Gómez have maintained, the form of reciprocal awareness implicit in communication of nonnatural meaning can also be realized in a nonverbal way. This can happen, for example, through the mechanism of attention—a mechanism fundamentally, albeit not exclusively, based on eye contact. First gazing to the desired object and then to the eyes of the interlocutor, nonverbal beings can create a chain of attention that has as many levels as those of metarepresentations and that can efficaciously attain the result desired from intentional communication. "Attention contact" is how Gómez defined the mechanism that consists in paying attention to the attention of the other who in turn pays attention to our attention.[34] Present also in children, preverbal communication based on eye contact has been noticed in animals in connection with various functions. While some respond to basic situations, such as the purely attentional function (to make one look in a certain direction) or the function of request (the so-called "begging" in circumstances of food-sharing, sexual allurement), others are quite sophisticated. According to some researchers, for example, chimpanzees who go out in patrols consult each other silently about the decisions to be made, and it also seems that the entire group uses silent communication to decide when to leave home and where to meet later.[35]

Overall, therefore, the Darwinian idea that human language is the natural extension of systems of signals existing in other animals has not only been recovered but also successfully defended in many recent studies. This added a final, decisive piece to the intellectual shift taking place. For if the work of many philosophers and ethologists has definitively brought about a crisis in the behaviorist idea of the unconscious animal, what the authors investigating nonhuman linguistic abilities have suggested is that even the direct access that has always been considered confined to our minds can sensibly be extended to the (once nonexistent) minds of animals.

Chapter 2

■■

The Problem of Moral Status

In a controversial volume published a few years ago, Alasdair Mac-Intyre criticizes the conception of the human being that he attributes to modernity, and in particular to the Enlightenment. Post-Enlightenment individuals, he maintains, are abstract and rootless. They are removed both from a worldview within which alone they could find their role and meaning, and from a web of actual relationships with other individuals, with a people and a tradition that might structure and shape them. More generally, MacIntyre attacks what he defines as "the conception of 'moral philosophy' as an independent and isolable area of enquiry."[1]

MacIntyre's cultural habitat is Anglo-American. His targets are therefore to be found within the analytical tradition. A conservative philosopher in the real sense of the term, he has recently made an important contribution to the revival of the oldest view of morality within Western philosophical tradition (and not only within it): that ethics of virtue that sees morality as a set of orientations for developing forms of excellence—forms that can be rooted only in a specific worldview.

Concretely, MacIntyre's target is emotivism, a metaethical theory that had considerable success during the period in which, as we have seen, logical positivism denied objective value to any statement that was not empirically verifiable (or falsifiable). Emotivists, accepting this approach, maintained that moral language, far from making statements that could be true or false, has merely the end—emotive, indeed—of influencing behavior. When he asserts that this renders impossible not only rational agreement but also moral debate, MacIntyre is not saying something new but rather something broadly agreed on. The problem is, however, that this objection is raised not only against emotivism but against all modern ethics, of which "the emotivist self"[2] becomes somehow the symbol. Basically, what MacIntyre claims is that the Enlightenment's twofold moral project—gradual detachment from any preconceived theological or metaphysical framework, and progressive replacement of the traditional network of specific connections with an anonymous social arena—has led ethics up a blind alley.

This is an interesting thesis because it presents quite clearly—albeit critically, and as if reversed in a mirror—the process of abstraction to which the rise of ethics as an autonomous discipline is generally ascribed. This process is not complete, however, and there are spheres of moral thinking where the contrast between the old and the new is particularly evident. One of them is the area concerned with determining the treatment of different beings. For while, where analytical philosophy is dominant, the inquiry focuses on the "moral status" of the beings involved, outside the English-speaking world appeal is still widely made to the notion of "ontological status"—a notion that is considered as foundational to that of moral status, or even directly substitutable for it.

Traditionally, in premodern philosophy, metaphysics predominates over ethics, which in the majority of authors is derived from the former. In most cases, ethics is based on values determined by a particular conception of being, and it is called on to realize a duty that already is within being and that issues from it.[3] Where we now tend to see a generic collection of autonomous beings without distinctions of sex, race, or aptitudes, traditional ethics perceives beings with fixed and differentiated natures, whose value and duties depend on the position they occupy within the world's hierarchy. It is difficult to understand the Aristotelian idea that the end of the free "man" is metaphysical contemplation while that of the slave is to please his master without sharing Aristotle's specific teleological worldview. And it is difficult to accept classic natural law without seeing human beings as the privileged fruit of a special creation, destined to play a part in a community transcendentally regulated by God. As Mary Warnock has emphasized, this sort of metaphysical approach still characterizes part of contemporary continental ethics, whose representatives remain primarily interested in constructing "large-scale, super-scientific explanations of things." Moral philosophy tends thus to be swallowed up into huge general systems built to explain the universe, and to be merely a "part of the general theory of man [*sic*], of human nature and its place in the universe."[4]

The phrase "ontological status" can be used in two ways. On the one hand, it can generically refer to the empirical characteristics of the being in question. Such meaning is certainly relevant to a practical discipline like ethics. On the other, however, the notion can be used in a sense according to which the ontological aspect is in the first place derived from a metaphysical interpretation of the world and is afterward set against the phenomenal aspect. In this case, the naturalistic constraint that science sets the limits of ontology is rejected in favor of metaphysical claims that transcend and are taken to override the results of empirical investigation.

To understand this point better, we can shift to a more concrete level. To what do those who inquire into the ontological status of a human embryo, as compared to that of a nonhuman animal, refer? Usually, they ask themselves two questions: first, What are the necessary constituting features of the entities that the embryo and the nonhuman in question are? and second, What is the position in the world of these specific entities? In other words, they seek to define the treatment of beings on the basis of a particular metaphysical account of their nature and of reality in general. The conclusion, normally, is that the embryo, since it is human, is rational by nature and is a kind of entity that should be treated as an end, and that the nonhuman, since she is a mere animal, is by nature irrational and is a kind of entity that may be treated as a means. It doesn't matter that the embryo is not even conscious and that the nonhuman may be quite rational: what is important is that the "ontological" (that is, metaphysical) nature of the beings is not affected by any "phenomenal" (that is, empirical) aspect. Neither does it matter that one could argue against the idea that rationality alone may grant the special dignity of being an end in itself: what is important is that, in the given metaphysical framework, the (allegedly) rational entities are at the top of the great chain of being.

In a sense, such an "ancillary" view of ethics, according to which moral philosophy should give up both empirical investigation and the use of its own theoretical tools in order to be at the service of an axiology of metaphysical descent, is not only older but also more archaic than the approaches that developed in the post-Enlightenment age. Like other fields of enquiry, ethics too has undergone deep theoretical changes. When, in 1874, Henry Sidgwick, recapitulating an intellectual path begun at least a century before, published *The Methods of Ethics,* the very title of his book was enough to show that ethics was not spared the critical period of self-reflection that marked the coming to maturity of a large number of disciplines. And it is once again Sidgwick who, by adopting the policy of keeping the nonethical commitments of moral philosophy to an absolute minimum, gives us the key to the importance of an emancipation from metaphysics.[5] For the fundamental point is that, in ethics as elsewhere, both the enquiry and the argumentation must be internal. Questions, concepts, methods, and principles must pertain to the field in question and meet its specific character.

What would we say now if, as happened for centuries in pre-Galilean physics, the tendency of water to flow downhill were to be explained with the fact that the "proper place" of water is down? Certainly we would object that explanatory categories are being used incorrectly. Science has long since rejected the idea that a descriptive explanation of nature can refer to a different realm such as that of values. And, as has rightly been emphasized, this transformation does not simply entail substituting one explanation for another but implies instead adopting a different kind of explanation that conforms to the peculiar character of the domain involved.[6] A similar problem can be found in ethics, and in particular in the context with which we are now concerned.

Roughly speaking, ethics has as its object two sorts of theory of conduct. Morality in the broad sense is an all-inclusive theory of conduct, which includes precepts about the good life, about the character traits to be fostered and the values to be pursued. It covers, in a sense, the domain of the supererogatory, that is, of what it might be good, but is not universally obligatory, to do or not to do; and it grants full significance to the existences of the members of particular moral worlds, instructing them about concrete understandings of the good life.

Morality in the narrow sense consists instead of a system of constraints on conduct, usually expressed in terms of negative duties, whose task is to protect the interests of individuals other than the agent. Essentially meant to counteract both active malevolence and selfishness, and linked to the domain covered by the golden rule, treat others as you would have them treat you, morality in the narrow sense plays a central role in contemporary ethical theories.[7] It is obviously prominent in approaches of Kantian descent, where respect for others imposes constraints on the freedom of the agent, but it appears also in the utilitarian tradition, usually reluctant to assess types of conduct a priori. To take a relevant example, John Stuart Mill, while discussing justice, does not fail to stress the primary importance of moral rules that prohibit individuals from harming each other.[8]

Questions of moral status directly concern morality in the narrow sense and lie therefore at the core of ethics. If, in the case of morality in the broad sense, the demand to pursue a specific conception of the good life may leave room for the arbitrariness of specific worldviews, when it comes to defining toward whom one should restrict one's conduct the requirement for justification is the most stringent, and, accordingly, appeals to undemonstrable metaphysical claims are the least acceptable. It is thus primarily to such context that one should refer Thomas Nagel's significant remark that ethics is a theoretical enquiry endowed with autonomous standards of justification and criticism, within which criteria coming from other domains have no direct relevance.[9]

All this should make apparent the significance of the notion of moral status. Its role is in fact twofold. On one side, the notion performs the fundamental function of pointing out that the arrangement of the different entities within the moral community should be categorized in specifically ethical terms. On the other, however, it can be more generically employed to shed light on specific answers to the question of which beings other than the agent should have their interests protected, and to what degree. It is in this latter sense that one can also speak of the moral status granted to the fetus, to women, or to nonhumans by religious doctrines or metaphysical accounts that contain no explicit notion of moral status. Every ethical approach includes—or presupposes—a theory of moral status, which is an essential part of value theory.[10] (From now on, when I use the notion of value, I will do it with reference to this sphere.) Further on, we will consider the criteria on which the main normative theories in western tradition have structured the moral community and the objections that can be raised against them. First, however, it is necessary to dwell on the more general aspects of the problem.

Moral Agents and Moral Patients

At the center of ethics, thus, lies a set of norms to govern behavior toward (at least some) other entities. Before asking which entities these are, it is necessary to clear the field of a possible source of confusion. According to a deep-rooted and widespread—though not always explicitly expressed—idea, ethics is to govern only certain beings, usually those that are rational and autonomous. This view may appear plausible but is in fact ambiguous. It can indeed mean two different things: (a) that only rational and autonomous beings can be morally responsible, or (b) that only what is done to rational and autonomous beings has moral weight. While the first claim might seem obvious, the second remains to be proven. Nonetheless, it is easy to transfer the plausibility of the former to the latter if one is not clear on the difference between the goal that is to be achieved by ethics and the way in which that goal is to be achieved, between the *what* and the *how* of ethics—if, in other words, one is not clear on a fundamental distinction: that between moral agents and moral patients.[11]

Previously, when considering the possible recipients of moral codes, I simply referred to agents. It is obvious that rules of behavior can only be addressed to beings that act—that make choices, that impinge on the external world. But to be an agent is not sufficient to qualify as a proper recipient of moral rules. One may be able to act without being able to understand, in a more or less abstract manner, the idea of right or wrong moral behavior. Ethical norms are thus addressed to a particular type of agent—the moral agent. In short, moral agents are those beings (rational, autonomous, etc.) which can reflect morally on how to act, and whose behavior can as a consequence be subject to moral evaluation. A moral agent, so long as she does not act under coercion, can be held accountable for her actions. This is what is usually the case with normal human beings over a certain age.

Long seen as unproblematic, the concept of moral agent has recently been subjected to revision. Steve Sapontzis, among others, has emphasized that the notion is gradational. Abstract reasoning, although essential for developing moral theories, is not required for direct and intentional moral action. The fully rational being, which is the quintessential form of the moral agent, able to understand and apply principles and norms, is part of a continuum. At the opposite end of this continuum there is the moral agent capable of being virtuous—whose conduct, that is, can be guided at least by an immediate perception of the interests of others, or by empathy with those who suffer, or by a courageous impulse. This redefinition opens the door to the possibility of seeing as moral agents, even though not in the full sense, children and many nonhuman beings.[12]

The problem that concerns us here, however, is another. When one speaks of moral status, it is to moral patients that one is referring. Asking, as we are doing, which are the entities other than the agent that should have their interests protected is tantamount to asking who is a moral patient. If the moral agent is a being whose *behavior* may be subject to moral evaluation, the moral patient is a being whose *treatment* may be subject to moral evaluation. More precisely, according to one of the first formulations of the concept, which we owe to G. J. Warnock, moral patients are those entities that are owed direct duties.[13]

It is apparent that not all beings are necessarily moral patients. Depending on the selected criterion, a greater or smaller number of entities will be excluded from moral consideration. Such entities have zero-grade moral status—they inhabit the no-man's-land surrounding the protected sphere of ethics. With them, one can do as one pleases: they are means to others' ends or, at best, objects of indifference. For most ethical theories, to shatter a stone or to mow the meadow's grass are wholly irrelevant actions. There have been, however, less obvious exclusions. In Mark Twain's *Huckleberry Finn,* Huck's aunt asks him whether the explosion of a steamboat's boiler harmed anyone. Huck says, "No'm: killed a nigger [*sic*]," to which the aunt replies with relief, "Well, it's lucky because sometimes people do get hurt."[14]

The protected sphere includes instead moral patients—the *others* of the golden rule, the beings which should be taken into account when deciding how to act (of course, moral agents too are moral patients when they are, so to speak, at the "recipient" end of the action). But how much do these beings matter? Are they all on the same level, or are there degrees as far as moral patiency is concerned? On this point, one can take either of two stands. According to the first, all the members of the moral community are equal—they deserve equal consideration, and their claims are equivalent. In some cases, the price to be paid for equality is a narrowing of the moral community, which becomes a sort of privileged club; but this is not an inevitable consequence. On the second view, on the other hand, moral patiency is no longer an all-or-nothing condition but admits of degrees. The moral community involves therefore a more or less complicated hierarchy, at the top of which there are the full members. On the whole, then, there are two kinds of dividing line: one concerns the inclusion in the moral community and draws a distinction between the beings that count and the ones that do not; the other is introduced in the case of a stratified moral community to define the comparative status of the beings within it.

With which kind of model does current morality fit? Clearly, what we are dealing with today is a stratified moral community. Both we and the members of other species belong in it, but while we are first-class moral patients, members of species other than *Homo sapiens* are confined to second-class status. Phrases such as "to love animals" and "to be kind to animals" well summarize an attitude based not on respect but on a more or less benevolent condescension.

And in fact, all the main aspects of difference in status come into play in our relationship with animals. First of all, a categorical element: animals are classified as the kinds of beings that can be subjected to a cost-benefit aggregative calculus without the protection of side constraints. In other words, in contrast to what happens with human beings, there is no limit to the sacrifices that can be inflicted on nonhuman individuals in the pursuit of a collective benefit (usually human). This means that animals can be used as mere means to others' ends—and not haphazardly the American philosopher Robert Nozick speaks of "utilitarianism for animals, Kantianism for people."[15] Second, a quantitative aspect: when the interests of humans and nonhumans are compared, the exchange rate is extremely high. Virtually every trivial human interest (except perhaps that in gratuitous cruelty) takes precedence over the vital interests of members of other species, who are harmed or killed even for matters of taste, entertainment, or curiosity. Finally, a substantive element: even in case animals are granted a (minimal) interest in welfare, the interest in living, which is the real key to full moral patiency, is confined to human beings.

In Search of the Criteria

On what grounds may such distinctions be drawn? In a volume devoted to the problem of abortion, Wayne Sumner discusses the question of criteria. In his view, both the inclusive and the comparative criteria ought (1) to be general, that is, applicable to any entity, and thus capable of resolving most (preferably all) questions of moral status; (2) to connect moral status to the empirical properties of the being; and (3) to be morally relevant.[16]

The first prerequisite, in itself evident, is worth emphasizing in view of the widespread tendency to set the problem of the treatment of the human fetus apart from other questions of moral status. The second is linked to the refusal of any appeal to alleged, and merely speculative, ontological characteristics: the properties on the basis of which a particular status is attributed must be empirical properties. Sumner defines this clearly:

> The function of a criterion is to distribute a certain moral [status] among the entities in the world in accordance with their possession or lack of certain properties. It cannot serve this function unless we have some independent means of ascertaining which entities possess the properties in question. These means will be empirical ones, since they are our normal means of discovering the (nonmoral) properties of objects in the world.[17]

The third prerequisite, finally, requires that the properties to which the criterion points have some plausible connection with the argumentation that is proper to the moral domain.

In this chapter, I will deal only with the question of the criteria of inclusion—that is, of the characteristics that make a being the recipient of direct duties. The problem of a possible hierarchy in levels of moral status, and hence of comparative criteria, will be taken up again in more detail later. While examining the main alternatives, I will bear in mind the three prerequisites for the acceptability of criteria suggested by Sumner: generality, connection with the empirical properties of the being, and moral relevance. To these, however, I will add a fourth, propounded by James Rachels and perhaps too rarely considered.

The aspect with which Rachels is concerned is the specification of the formal principle of equality, according to which individuals are to be treated in the same way unless there is a relevant difference between them that justifies a difference in treatment. But what is a relevant difference? To answer this question, Rachels resorts to an example. Suppose, he says, that an admissions committee that has admitted applicant A and rejected applicant B explains that A's college grades were excellent while B's grades were poor. Then, suppose that a doctor who has given a shot of penicillin to patient A and has put in a cast the arm of patient B explains that A had an infection and B had a broken arm. So far so good. Now, imagine we switch things around. Suppose that the admissions committee, when asked to justify admitting A while rejecting B, replies that A had an infection and B had a broken arm, and that the doctor justifies his choice of the shot for A and the cast for B by claiming that A had better college grades than B. Why do these answers sound silly? Obviously because what is relevant in the one context is irrelevant in the other. Rachels's conclusion is that whether a difference between individuals justifies a difference in treatment depends on the kind of treatment that is in question. A difference that justifies one kind of difference in treatment need not justify another.[18]

Recast in terms of the prerequisites of a plausible criterion of moral status, this means that it is not enough for the criterion, be it inclusive or comparative, to be rooted in a moral theory to be considered as relevant. In addition to moral relevance, there must be a connection between proposed status and adopted criterion. In other words, the criterion must possess a form of relevance that we could define as *contextual*.

Inclusion in the Moral Community

What then, are the criteria for inclusion in the moral community that can somehow meet such prerequisites? Of course, many are the lists of necessary and sufficient conditions for inclusion proposed by different scholars. Sumner takes into consideration four criteria: being intrinsically valuable; being alive; being sentient, or, to use a more traditional term, being conscious[19]; and being rational. Other authors add: being potentially rational or potentially a person; and being a person. The criterion of membership in the human species, which we have already mentioned in connection with the sanctity-of-life doctrine, deserves a special discussion, both for the particular problems it implies and for its pervasiveness. It will thus be examined separately. The new field of environmental ethics, on the other hand—provided that the notion of moral status is not altogether rejected, as is the case with deep ecologists—suggests a further possibility, of which the position of J. Baird Callicott in his early articles may be representative. Recasting in more theoretical terms the "land ethic" of the American conservationist Aldo Leopold, Callicott locates the ultimate value in the biotic community, and he assigns all the entities that belong in it a widespread and unstable moral status, dependent on their contribution to the "integrity, stability, and beauty" of the whole.[20] Although later Callicott has mitigated his ecocentrism, the criterion of the contribution to the functioning of the biotic community remains a good example of a holistic approach to the problem of moral status.

On the whole, therefore, we have a list, if not exhaustive at least representative, that could be rearranged in the following way: playing a role in the biotic community; being alive; being intrinsically valuable; being conscious; being potentially rational; being potentially a person; being rational; and being a person. Obviously, different criteria select different sets of beings. Our list has a funnel-like structure, which starts from the most inclusive standards and then reaches maximum selectivity. We can roughly divide it into two principal areas. The first one centers on manifestations of subjectivity. It is composed of consciousness, rationality, and personhood. The second one—consisting of role in the biotic community and organic life—appeals somehow to objective theories, referring to conditions or factors that are independent of the subjective experience of the individual.[21] The requisites of intrinsic value, potential rationality, and potential personhood are instead ambiguous and seem to lie in an intermediate sphere between the two areas.

Why opt for this kind of classification? Because a crucial problem underlies it. Imaginative identification is usually seen as the key instrument of ethics, so much so that it is defined as "the primary form of moral argument."[22] To put oneself in the shoes of others allows one to (attempt to) understand how they may be affected by what happens to them. But can one try, for example, as Leopold suggests, to "think like a mountain"?[23] In spite of what some advocates of the land ethic maintain, it seems that imaginative identification cannot play any role here. All the more so: the application of the role-shift test that underlies the golden rule leads to the result of excluding non-conscious entities from the moral community, since if we put ourselves in their shoes, what we find is a complete blank.[24] This points toward the immediate elimination of the two criteria—role in the biotic community and organic life—that appeal to objective theories.

Against this conclusion, a criticism might be raised. The argument just developed, it might be claimed, is plainly circular. For if one starts from a criterion designed to reckon with subjectivity, it is natural that its application should lead to the exclusion of what lies beyond the limits of subjectivity. But the problem is whether it is necessary in the first place to reckon with subjectivity. If this weren't the case—if it were not necessary to insist on holding that the essence of moral agency lies in putting oneself in the shoes of any possible moral patient—then the traditional limits of ethics should be broken open on behalf of a new approach, which might be able to harbor concern for all living organisms or even for ecosystems with all the nonliving entities they include.

The objection hits the mark, but only in the sense that it pushes the problem onto a higher level. The true question is thus: Why start from a criterion based on subjectivity? If there are good reasons for doing so, then, far from being circular, the argument becomes just a step in a longer line of reasoning. In what sense, then, is it important that the criterion be rooted in subjectivity? The answer is, I believe, simple. The value we are looking for—a value that can set limits on the behavior of moral agents—is both fundamental and general. It is fundamental because it makes the being that possesses it a moral patient, removing it from the grey area of the entities that can prima facie be ignored, consumed, or exploited. It is general because it must be accepted by all moral agents, whatever their conception of the good life and of the goals to be achieved in living it. As a consequence, the foundation of such a value must be deep and uncontroversial. Now, the only value endowed with these characteristics is the value that subjectivity ascribes to the presence of positive experiences (or to the absence of negative experiences) and, all in all, either directly or indirectly, to itself. In other words, besides embodying a point of view on the world, the subject is also a direct and immediate source of normativity.[25] This is the kernel of truth that—albeit in a distorted way, as we shall see later—usually lies in procedural, discursive, and, in part, contractarian ethical perspectives. The basic idea is that the value—the normativity—of the subject must set limits on what can be done to it and imposed on it.

On the contrary, all the theories of moral status not rooted in subjectivity must face a serious problem of justification. Albert Schweitzer, defending his well-known ethics of "reverence for life," writes that the truly moral being does not need to ask whether this or that life is capable of feeling: "Life as such is sacred to him. He tears no leaf from a tree, plucks no flower. . . ." William Frankena, among others, rejoins: "Why, if leaves and trees have no capacity to feel pleasure or to suffer, should I tear no leaf from a tree?"[26] In other words, if, when we consider how a certain being is affected by our actions, we become aware that the being cannot care about what we do, why should we restrict our behavior? If the beings involved have no positive or negative attitudes toward their treatment, who or what has the authority to tell us that we should act toward them in one way rather than another? It is in this sense that every approach that overrides the authority of the individual tends to wax "metaphysical."[27] Only a general conception of being seems to be able to provide sufficient justification for the introduction into the moral community of a being without subjectivity.

This raises the suspicion that environmental ethics may not be as novel as it would like to appear. Whether the selected criterion is that of playing a role in the biotic community (which is characteristic of holistic perspectives) or that of being alive (which is instead the case with atomistic approaches),[28] it seems that what we are dealing with are new versions of the traditional approach, which arbitrarily draws universal values from specific worldviews.

With this, many environmental philosophers would disagree. They would probably object that such a presentation of their views is not fair because, if it is true that what they put forward are interpretations of the world, we are not for this reason dealing with metaphysical appeals. It is from science that in most though not all cases environmental ethics draws its understanding of reality. And science is the universal and objective theoretical discourse par excellence. Now, let's accept for the sake of argument that this is the case—that science actually is an objective and universal discourse and that it can offer an overall interpretation of reality without any recourse to metaphysical elements. This doesn't in any way prevent environmental theories that draw inspiration from scientific views from running into a further, serious difficulty—the problem of the distinction between facts and values. "The introduction of [notions which combine the ideal with the actual]," writes Sidgwick, "into Ethics is liable to bring with it a fundamental confusion between 'what is' and 'what ought to be,' destructive of all clearness in ethical reasoning."[29] Sidgwick's observation somehow echoes David Hume's famous point:

> In every system of morality, which I have hitherto met with, I have always remarked that the author proceeds for some time in the ordinary way of reasoning, and establishes the being of a God, or makes observations concerning human affairs; when of a sudden I am surprised to find, that instead of the usual copulations of propositions, *is,* and *is not,* I meet with no proposition that is not connected with an *ought,* or an *ought not.* This change is imperceptible; but is, however, of the last consequence. For as this *ought,* or *ought not,* expresses some new relation or affirmation, 'tis necessary that it should be observed and explained; and at the same time that a reason should be given, for what seems altogether inconceivable, how this new relation can be a deduction from others, which are entirely different from it.[30]

Accepting this general logical point, better known as Hume's Law, most contemporary moral philosophers reject the possibility of drawing prescriptive conclusions from descriptive premises. Since the attribution of moral status is the most basic form of value ascription, it seems that Hume's Law stands squarely in the way of the attempt to structure the moral community on the basis of the (alleged) scientific facts from which some versions of environmental ethics are guided.[31]

Can the requirement of the possession of intrinsic value—a requirement that is more or less prominently present in many defenses of objective theories but can as well be introduced in support of criteria connected to subjectivity—overcome these problems? Though the notion of intrinsic value may also be used with reference to mental states or states of affairs, here we are only interested in its use in reference to beings in the context of the problem of moral status. What does it mean to say of a being—for example, a natural object—that it has intrinsic value? Basically, it means to affirm that the value of the being is not bestowed from outside but is an integral part of the being itself. A common correlate of this idea is that beings that have intrinsic value can never be used simply as means, that is, that intrinsic value can never be fully reduced to instrumental value. On this view, if it can be claimed of an entity that it is intrinsically valuable, its treatment will be subject to direct constraints, and the entity in question will be introduced in the moral community.

The problem, however, is how such a claim can be justified. Not always do the authors who appeal to intrinsic value clearly tackle this problem, and sometimes mere postulation is seen as sufficient. J. Baird Callicott is an exception. He makes an interesting attempt to offer a foundation:

> But if we prove to be good for nothing, we believe, nevertheless, that we are still entitled to life, to liberty, to the pursuit of happiness. . . . Human dignity and the respect it commands—human ethical entitlement—are grounded ultimately in our claim to possess intrinsic value. Call this the phenomenological proof for the existence of intrinsic value. The question How do we know that intrinsic value exists? is similar to the question How do we know that consciousness exists? We experience both consciousness and intrinsic value introspectively and irrefutably.[32]

This passage is revealing because it lays bare the ambiguity that characterizes the notion. Intrinsic value turns out to be a sort of external projection—a hypostatization—of the value that the subject attributes to itself. But, on the one hand, for subjectivity the notion is redundant. And, on the other, once projected outside the subject, intrinsic value loses its "introspective and irrefutable" foundation, and must once again appeal to a specific worldview (be it metaphysical or scientific) that can ground it. In spite of its apparent role of bridge between the sphere of subjectivity and the sphere of objectivity, therefore, the criterion of intrinsic value appears to lead us back to the same difficulties we pointed out in the case of the requisites of being alive and having a role in the biotic community.

The exclusion of the appeal to the notion of intrinsic value brings with it the elimination from our list of a further item, in which such a notion covertly plays a role—the criterion of potential rationality. At first sight, the requirement of potential rationality seems to be connected to subjectivity. But this feeling, which is due to the involvement of a psychological characteristic like rationality, is called into doubt by the problem of potentiality. What does it mean to be potentially rational? It means not being actually so. The temporal discrepancy breaks off the link between rationality and subjectivity: it is not necessary to be actually a subject in order to be potentially rational. Small children are potentially rational subjects, but potential rationality is also predicated of embryos, that is, of nonconscious entities. This makes clear that, according to the criterion involved, rationality does not count insofar as it can influence subjectivity—for example, by affecting the results of the role-shift test—but counts instead in itself. The only way to defend this view lies, I believe, in ascribing intrinsic value to rationality. But the surreptitious introduction of intrinsic value cannot but raise once again the problems of justification we have already met with—and this in an especially counterintuitive way since, according to this criterion, to destroy an embryo can be, *ceteris paribus,* as wrong as killing a small child.

Given that an analogous argument can be developed regarding potential personhood, our initial list is now much reduced. In fact, only three contenders remain: being conscious, being rational, and being a person. All these criteria seem to meet the prerequisites of generality, connection with the empirical properties of the being, and moral relevance. (Some problems that arise in relation to the definition of person will be considered later. In this context I will keep to the current idea that to be a person means to possess one or more favored psychological characteristics, and when necessary, for the sake of brevity, I will translate the concept into the possession of the most often cited among them, that is, self-consciousness.) But what about the prerequisite of contextual relevance? Let us recall that the problem here is simply that of inclusion in the moral community, not that of the degree of inclusion. That is to say, what is under discussion is the criterion for being a moral patient—for counting for something—not the criterion for having special moral status.

What are, in short, the differences in treatment between those who count and those who do not count? Concretely, what is it like for a subject not to count at all? Apart from any possible nuances, not to count means once again to be liable to be reduced to nothing more than an instrument for fulfilling the ends of others. It means that one's interests, both trivial and vital, can be overridden for the slightest reason, or even for no reason at all. Let us try, then, to reexamine in this light the criterion of consciousness, that of rationality and that of personhood.

The first one is the minimal criterion of subjectivity: subjectivity begins where consciousness begins.[33] To be conscious means to have experiences and *to care* about these experiences. It means to have at least the interest in avoiding pain and experiencing pleasure. The adoption of this criterion implies therefore that subjectivity is never ignored.

The situation is different for the other two criteria. According to them, there are conscious beings that, due to the lack of a single capacity, or even of a cluster of capacities, are thoroughly excluded from the role-shift test. But this is highly implausible. One might perhaps argue that the presence of particular psychological characteristics can influence possible *levels* in moral status—this is something we will consider further on—but it is not reasonable to maintain that the absence of these characteristics may sanction the absolute exclusion from the moral community of beings that are endowed with subjectivity. What may rationality or the possession of self-consciousness have to do with having conscious interests (henceforth, simply interests)? From a logical point of view, it seems that there is no cogent reason for refusing to take into consideration any interest that imaginative identification makes it possible to determine, whatever the other characteristics of the beings in question.

Such is indeed the conclusion that most authors reach. This conclusion can be called into question in two ways. In the first place, one might release the criteria of rationality and personhood from the relationship with subjectivity and interpret them in objectivistic terms. This can be effected by assigning intrinsic value to rationality and personhood. We can exclude this move because, as we have already shown, it would run into the problems that affect the notion of intrinsic value. Second, one might grant to rationality and personhood a particular kind of instrumental value. The idea is that the attribution of moral status can be justified by means of intersubjective agreement. In order to be motivated to reach an agreement, one must benefit from the agreement, and consequently each participant will impose as a condition the recognition of her own value. But in order to abide by the agreement one must be rational, or self-conscious. The agreement will therefore include only rational or self-conscious beings, who will turn out to be the sole entities endowed with moral status. Merely conscious beings will thus be excluded from the moral community.

Much simplified, this is the basic structure of some forms of contractarianism based on reciprocity. Is it an acceptable position? One can doubt it. At the center of such versions of contractarian theory lies the attempt to offer a justification for the value of the subject that may at the same time be a motivation for its recognition. David Gauthier, one of the most authoritative defenders of this approach, after stating that his aim is to provide a reconstruction of morality "to be substituted for obsolete appeals to intrinsic value," adds: "I connect the idea of impartiality to the idea of equal individual rationality"— where rationality means self-interest.[34] Now, one may or may not agree on the attempt to link morality to self-interest, but it is nonetheless difficult to understand how being impartial is compatible with the fact of completely ignoring the interests of subjects who are unable to reciprocate. Rational contractors gain no advantage from accepting principles that offer guarantees to individuals such as nonhumans or severely disabled humans, who are unable to give any guarantee in return. But if the golden rule is replaced by what we might call the silver rule, "treat others as they would treat you," [35] mutual advantage has the devastating effect of driving ethical impartiality off the stage.

If even this defense of the possible role of the requirements of rationality and personhood fails, it seems that the criterion of consciousness remains the only plausible candidate with respect to the access to the status of moral patient. As the philosopher of mind Colin McGinn sums it up, "The primary object of moral respect is precisely the self—that to which experiences happen. . . . The moral community is the community of selves."[36] This is also, by and large, the position of contemporary morality. It is indeed widely accepted that both nonhumans and humans with serious mental disabilities endowed with interests are included in the moral community. From this common basis, therefore, the discussion of possible comparative levels within the moral community can be set going. But, first, it is worth the trouble to consider briefly the way questions of moral status have been dealt with by mainstream Western philosophy, and how we got where we are.

Chapter 3

■■

The Traditional Accounts

Beliefs about the treatment of nonhuman animals have always been part of our cultural history. Their development, however, was not a linear one, starting from an exclusive stance and then reaching, gradually, an ever broader moral concern. Rather, different views made their appearance, became marginal, and then reappeared in the course of centuries.

Instead of following an often convoluted route, then, it may be useful to focus on the most influential positions, preferring a critical analysis based on structural characteristics rather than a historical reconstruction. Thus, bearing in mind the results of the previous chapter, we will examine in turn three positions: the view that denies animals any form of moral consideration; the view that, while excluding them from the moral community, maintains that there exist indirect duties toward them; and the view that includes them among moral patients.

Absolute Dismissal, or Descartes and God's Clocks

However strange it may seem, the total exclusion of nonhumans from the ethical sphere (the "absolute nadir" as far as their moral status is concerned[1]) was formulated relatively late in the history of Western philosophy. When in the first half of the seventeenth century René Descartes seeks to reconcile classical metaphysics with nascent scientific rationalism, what emerges is a radically dichotomic worldview. On one side, the old world, represented by the rational soul—a world Descartes clearly states he does not want to subvert, stressing his commitment to adhere "constantly to the religion in which by God's grace [he] had been instructed since [his] childhood."[2] The rational soul is immortal and is "a substance the whole *essence* or nature of which is to think and [for whose] existence there is no need of any place, nor does it depend on any material thing."[3] On the other side, the new mechanistic explanation of nature, which is seen as mere matter subject to laws and interpretable only in terms of cause and effect. It is to this sphere that human and nonhuman bodies belong: though inhabited by animal spirits that like "a very subtle wind"[4] govern all their vital activities, they remain matter devoid of consciousness.

As a hybrid composed of soul and body, not foreign to nature but placed above it via the presence of the soul or *cogito*, the human being is a sort of bridge between the two worlds. Nonhumans, on the contrary, wholly belong in the sphere of brute matter—something that means not only that they are entirely subject to deterministic principles but also that they lack any form of subjectivity. Cartesian essentialism doesn't admit of degrees, but, after the scholastic fashion, it implies that "the question of more or less occurs only in the sphere of the *accidents* and does not affect the *forms* or natures."[5] In an age when mechanical clocks arouse wonder and admiration, Descartes describes the "brutes" as mere natural automata, that act mechanically "like a clock which tells the time better than our judgement does."[6] Nor should we be struck by their apparent abilities or by their possible writhings and twistings: insofar as they are automata created by God, animals are incomparably better regulated than any device human beings might devise.

As we have already noticed in the case of behaviorism, the denial of any form of animal subjectivity offers some advantages from the moral point of view. If nonhuman animals are nothing but machines, human beings can do with them as they wish. It is no accident, therefore, that the growing practice of "vivisection"—that is, the dissection of live animals—gained both practical boost and ethical legitimation from the Cartesian stance. Descartes himself practiced it as a physiologist, and many vivisectionists of the time declared themselves his followers. While the analogy with mechanical clocks was widely used to scorn any moral qualms, Descartes showed that he was well aware of the implications of his view:

> Thus my opinion is not so much cruel to animals as indulgent to men . . . since it absolves them from the suspicion of crime when they eat or kill animals.[7]

What is one to say about Descartes's position? Apparently, the Cartesian criterion for inclusion in the moral community is the presence of subjectivity—and, from a philosophical point of view, the idea that where there is no subjectivity there is nothing to take morally into consideration appears sound. The problem seems therefore to be the following: on what grounds can one deny to nonhumans that subjectivity which is so easily attributed to all human beings? The Cartesian approach seems to identify rationality and subjectivity: "animal spirits" are not enough to secure any form of consciousness. Further, rationality is also identified with the immortal soul.

The criterion of inclusion thus takes on a different character. From an empirically verifiable characteristic such as rationality, we have shifted to a metaphysical notion such as that of immortal soul. Since the appeal to the possession of an immortal soul breaks the connection between moral status and the empirical properties of beings, this feature of the Cartesian approach fails to meet one of the basic prerequisites for the acceptability of criteria of moral status and must as a consequence be set aside. Along with it, we must forget the remarks passed off as decisive in the *Discourse on the Method,* according to which, after the denial of God, the utmost error is "to imagine that the soul of the brute is of the same nature as our own, and that in consequence, after this life we have nothing to fear, or to hope for, any more than the flies and ants." [8]

Even if we do not consider the introduction of metaphysical elements, however, Descartes's criterion presents serious problems. First, there is the factual question of the alleged radical discontinuity between humans and nonhumans as far as the presence of rationality is concerned. Today, the notion of distinct and immutable natures is seen as obsolete. After the discovery of evolution, it is no longer possible to defend any version of Cartesian essentialism. Evolutionary biology has swept away the idea that there is an ontological gulf between our species and the others, clearly stating that the way in which individuals are grouped—in species, varieties, and so on—is more or less arbitrary. But even before Darwin the elements of continuity were evident. Aristotle, while drawing a radical distinction between humans and nonhumans (but also, for that matter, between free human beings and slaves), maintained that animals had their own peculiar pleasures.[9] All Greek philosophy is crossed by a strand of thought that does not see a clear separation between us and, literally, "the other en-souled ones."[10] Descartes was well aware of this, as he was acquainted with the defense of continuity put forward by Montaigne.[11] It is to the attempt to get around this problem that one should probably attribute his appeals to the scholastic approach based on ontological gaps. And it is still in this light that one may see his choice to raise the use of language to the status of sole certain indicator of the presence of rationality. But even apart from the already considered question of linguistic abilities, it is difficult to maintain that a capacity as complex as rationality must reveal itself only in a single way. Undoubtedly, language is both an important means for communicating thought and a sign of the presence of sophisticated intellectual abilities. Nonetheless, as developmental psychology as well bears out, rationality, far from being an all-or-nothing characteristic, is a many-sided and complex capacity that cannot be identified by a single criterion.

But let us grant, for the sake of argument, that all nonhuman animals lack rationality. Descartes would still have to demonstrate that rationality is a necessary requisite for subjectivity—and this without the *deus ex machina* represented by the immortal soul. The undertaking is not only counterintuitive—since it means denying that not merely nonhumans but also, for example, little children have any point of view on the world (that is, that they *care* about what happens to them)—but is also theoretically unlikely. To make rationality and subjectivity thoroughly coincide is to assert the impossibility of any form of conscious experience in the absence of reason. Without the support of the metaphysical distinction between *res cogitans* and *res extensa,* the notion of subjectivity proposed by Descartes becomes extremely implausible. Accordingly, the inclusive criterion based on this notion is radically undermined.

Updating Descartes?

After Darwin, it might seem unlikely that there could be a theoretical restatement of an essentialist dualism such as that of Descartes. Such a revival, however, did in fact occur in recent years. Not haphazardly defined as the "neo-Cartesian" revival, this approach brings the animal-machine back on the scene (although no longer with God playing the watchmaker), maintaining, once again in radical contrast with common sense, that the experiences of nonhumans, suffering included, cannot be proper objects of moral consideration because, unlike humans, nonhumans lack any form of self-awareness. For example, Peter Carruthers, author of the best-known formulation of this view, states that animals are not conscious because a conscious mental state, as opposed to a nonconscious one, is a mental state available to conscious thought—where a conscious thought is an event that is available to be consciously thought about in turn.[12]

Underscoring both the manifest circularity of such a definition of conscious thought and the disputability of the assumption that nonhuman animals are devoid of thought, many authors have called into question the essential premises of Carruthers's view. But even if one sets aside these problems, there still is obviously the question of how an approach based on abrupt fractures between phylogenetically contiguous beings can be reconciled with evolutionary theory. To some degree aware of this difficulty, Carruthers endeavors to put forward a hypothesis. He claims, namely, that it was just the adaptive value connected to the ability to predict and explain, and thus to manipulate and direct, the behavior of others that gave rise in humans, and only humans, to the capacity for second-order thoughts (or thoughts about thoughts).[13] This answer, however, does nothing but reintroduce in other terms the difficulties it aims at solving. It is in fact difficult to imagine how wholly unconscious beings might suddenly evolve such capacities, abruptly starting to think and reason about the beliefs, desires, intentions, and experiences of others.[14] Given the burden of proof that a view having so little compatibility with a fundamental aspect of our web of beliefs must meet, Carruthers, like Descartes, appears to be quite far from providing a satisfactory justification of his position.

Carruthers's approach shares with the Cartesian stance the idea that there is a radical dichotomy between us and the members of other species. It clearly parts from it, however, in focusing only on the mechanisms of consciousness. There exists, though, within current philosophical theory, a further view that, while coming to less extreme conclusions about the animal mind, attempts to retrieve directly from Descartes a central role for language as a capacity differentiating humans and nonhumans. According to the American philosopher Raymond Frey, linguistic ability, far from being only one faculty among others, is rather a prerequisite for the exercise of a fundamental psychological activity such as that of believing. This activity, in turn, is necessary to be able to desire.[15] The underlying idea is that to believe, for example, that a friend is at the door, means to believe that the statement "a friend is at the door" is true. On the basis of this interpretation of the structure of beliefs, animals, lacking a human language, are, if not automata, at least extremely rudimentary beings who cannot even be compared with the members of our species.

Put forward in slightly different versions as well, such a view has been criticized by, among others, John Searle. After claiming that it is a mistake to see mental phenomena such as beliefs as dependent on language, Searle remarks that "true" and "false," while being indeed metalinguistic predicates, are more fundamentally *metaintentional* predicates, used to assess success and failure of representations to achieve fit in the mind-to-world direction of fit. As a consequence,

> for neither beliefs nor desires does the animal require a language; rather what she requires is some device for recognizing whether the world is the way it seemed to be (belief) and whether the world is the way the animal wants it to be (desire).[16]

Searle makes this point clear by way of an example. Why is the dog barking up the tree? Because he *believes* that the cat is up the tree, and he wants to catch up to her. Why does he believe the cat is up the tree? Because he *saw* her run up the tree. Why does he now stop barking up the tree and start running toward the neighbors' yard? Because he no longer believes that the cat is up the tree, but in the neighbors' yard. And why did he correct his belief? Because he just saw—and no doubt smelled—the cat run there; and *seeing and smelling is believing*. The general point, Searle argues, is that animals correct their beliefs all the time on the basis of their perceptions. In order to make these corrections, they have to be able to distinguish the state of affairs in which their beliefs are satisfied from the one in which they are not satisfied. And what goes for beliefs goes for desires as well.[17]

The conclusion that nonhumans not only, contra Carruthers, are conscious but also, contra Frey, have beliefs and desires is of course in line with folk psychology, that habitually and confidently employs mentalistic language with respect to them. Those who have observed free-living animals, and even more so those who live with animals, wouldn't in the least doubt the resemblance between their minds and ours. To return to Searle, in a less formal version:

> Why . . . am I so confident that my dog, Ludwig Wittgenstein, is con-
> scious? Well, why is he so confident I am conscious? I think part of
> the correct answer, in the case of both Ludwig and me, is that any
> other possibility is out of the question. We have, for example, known
> each other now for quite a while so there is not really any possibility
> of doubt.[18]

If neither Carruthers's thesis about the relationship between consciousness and self-consciousness nor Frey's thesis about the relationship between language and belief withstand criticism, the (already
improbable) contemporary attempt to revive Cartesianism can be considered as thoroughly unsuccessful.

The Superiority of Rational Nature: How Kant Created Humanism

In the *Lectures on Ethics,* Kant states:

> So far as animals are concerned, we have no direct duties. Animals are
> not self-conscious and are there merely as means to an end. That end
> is man. . . . Our duties towards animals are merely indirect duties to-
> wards humanity. Animal nature has analogies to human nature, and
> by doing our duties to animals in respect of manifestations of human
> nature, we indirectly do our duty towards humanity.[19]

In the idea that nonhumans are nothing but means one can perceive
echoes of Aristotle: "the other animals [exist] for the good of man, the
domestic species both for his service and for his food, and . . . most
of the wild ones for the sake of his food and of his supplies of other
kinds."[20] And the thesis of indirect duties betrays a reminiscence of
Thomas Aquinas's remarks on the subject of biblical injunctions
against cruelty to nonhumans: "this is . . . to remove man's thoughts
from being cruel to other men, and lest through being cruel to animals
one become cruel to human beings."[21]

These short quotations contain in a nutshell the elements of the
most enduring and pervasive thesis about the treatment of nonhumans
in all Western culture. In short: animals, as mere means, have zero
grade moral status—that is, they are excluded from the moral community. However, there are limits to what moral agents can do to
them. Such limits are dictated by the fact that our behavior toward

animals can rebound upon our behavior toward the only true moral patients, namely, other human beings.

What is surprising is that the thesis persisted so long even though its justifications and context constantly changed. In fact, we meet it again almost unchanged at the beginning of the twentieth century when, for example, the Jesuit Joseph Rickaby claims that as "brute beasts" are like things for us, and as they exist for us and not for themselves, "we do right in using them unsparingly for our need and convenience"[22]—with the exception, once again, of the prohibition of gratuitous cruelty, which might induce us to become cruel to humans as well.

Why are human beings ends in themselves, whereas nonhumans are means to human ends? In both Aristotelian ethics and Aquinas's doctrine, the metaphysical element is decisive. To establish the view that nonhuman beings were made for "man," the Greek philosopher appeals to nature, which makes nothing purposeless or in vain, and the Christian theologian refers back to God, who doesn't want them "for their own sake, but for another's"[23] (ours, that is). In both cases, however, the requisite of rationality is prominent: means are those beings that do not share in reason, viz., irrational creatures. Such requisite acquires an even more central role in Kantian doctrine.

Kant's thought too has a strong metaphysical component, however, and it is thus necessary to set apart this aspect from the rest of his doctrine. Hence, we won't take into account the three postulates of immortality, freedom, and the existence of God. In particular, what we must set aside in order to bring the Kantian criterion within the terms of the prerequisites of acceptability we have determined is the implication of the second postulate, according to which freedom is linked to the cosmological idea of an "intelligible world" and to the awareness of the existence of rational beings within it.

Cruelty and Indirect Duties

If we bring Kantian reason back to Earth—if, that is, as suggested by the German philosopher Ursula Wolf, we substitute an empirical notion for the metaphysical notion of reason[24]—what we are confronted by is a version of the criterion of rationality for the inclusion in the moral community. Since, as we have emphasized, all inclusive criteria that appeal to anything beyond mere consciousness have to reckon with the prerequisite of contextual relevance, our question is,

Can Kant's elaborate arguments overcome the preliminary argument according to which is implausible for the lack of *a single capacity* to justify a difference in treatment as *fundamental* as that implied by the exclusion from the moral community?

Kant, unlike Descartes, considers nonhumans as conscious beings. In the excerpt from the *Lectures* quoted above, after observing that animals possess a nature that has analogies to human nature, he states:

> Thus, if a dog has served his master long and faithfully, his service, on the analogy of human service, deserves reward, and when the dog has grown too old to serve, his master ought to keep him until he dies.[25]

However, for those then swayed to believe that, since what we praise is *his* behavior, we might eventually have direct duties toward the dog, Kant hastens to add:

> If a man shoots his dog because the animal is no longer capable of service, he does not fail in his duty to the dog, for the dog cannot judge, but his act is inhuman and damages in himself that humanity which it is his duty to show towards mankind. If he is not to stifle his human feelings, he must practise kindness towards animals, for he who is cruel to animals becomes hard also in his dealings with men.[26]

One cannot help being puzzled by this passage. First and foremost, what about the idea that one cannot infringe her duties toward a being in case the being in question "cannot judge"? Consider: a mentally disabled child behaves generously toward her "normal" companions—should the companions be grateful to her, or should they treat her well in order that they don't start to treat each other badly? Or else: a person benefitted us in the past and is now irredeemably senile but needs our help: should we reciprocate on account of what she did for us or merely for fear of becoming ungrateful toward those who can understand our gratitude? When it is a matter of acquired duties, that is, duties arising from specific interactions between individuals— here between the faithful dog and his "master"—logic requires that they refer directly to the individuals involved.

The situation is different when it comes to unacquired duties, which hold irrespective of any interactions or even institutional arrangements. If ever there is an unacquired duty, it is certainly the duty not to be cruel. And this is a further source of puzzlement. At first sight, the notion of cruelty appears to be closely connected to the harm suffered by the object of the treatment. As a consequence, it seems that it is not logically possible to speak of cruelty in relation to a being that is not *already* the object of direct duties. It could be a second-class moral patient, but it has to be a moral patient—there are no injunctions against cruelty toward stones. This is confirmed by the fact that Kant, while locating nonhumans and stones in the same category, that of *things,* does not urge us not to maltreat stones lest this might damage our humanity toward "mankind." Hence, there are two alternatives: either "animal nature has analogies to human nature" in a morally relevant sense, and the risk of passing from cruelty toward nonhumans to cruelty toward humans arises from the fact that in the former case as well we violate direct duties, although perhaps less stringent; or nonhumans, as mere means, have no moral weight, and then there is no ground—in their case as in the case of stones—for the fear that a certain kind of behavior could rebound upon the behavior toward the only beings that matter morally, namely, the ends in themselves. All the more so: as it has been remarked, Kant is not even theoretically capable of distinguishing between permissible and impermissible treatment of beings that are not ends in themselves, because "we are certainly acting rationally in treating as a means what has value merely as a means."[27]

Ends and Means

There is, however, a possibility of avoiding all these contradictions. It lies in doing away with the idea of indirect duties in favor of a view closer to that of Descartes. And it is no coincidence that the *Lectures,* transcribed by students, antedate by a few years Kant's major works on morality,[28] where the dichotomies *rational being–non-rational being* and *end-in-itself–means to others' ends* seem in fact decidedly to prevail over any possible analogy. This takes us straight back to the fundamental question: Why are rational beings ends in themselves, while nonrational beings are means to others' ends? In what exactly do the role and significance of reason lie? Put most briefly, Kant's argument seems to be the following.

Beings endowed with reason are free because they create their own laws. Since moral law, in order to exist, requires freedom, it is reason that makes morality possible. But a moral law based on reason cannot be particular and subjective: it must be generally and objectively valid for all rational beings. The imperative through which such law expresses itself, therefore, cannot be hypothetical, that is, dependent on specific objectives, as happens in the case of sciences or of the pru-

dential search for happiness, where instrumental rationalty rules—
"*if* you want that, *then* do this." It will be, on the contrary, a categorical imperative, that is, an imperative released from any specific
content and characterized only by the form of universality that reason itself imposes on it. The imperative of morality, in other words,
will contain nothing but the necessity of conformity to a universally
valid law. From this, the first and most famous formulation of the categorical imperative: *Act only according to that maxim by which you
can at the same time will that it should become a universal law.*[29]

Apparently, nothing in this formulation makes reference to a distinction between the recipients of the action. The distinction between
ends and means concerns only actions and their objectives or motives,
and the founding role attributed to reason seems to have generated a
formal mechanism for the production of moral judgments universally
applicable, and without effects as far as the moral community is concerned. But the Kantian account of the centrality of reason does not
stop here.

Remarking that what the will needs as a principle for its self-
determination is an end, Kant adds in fact that while hypothetical
imperatives, which are subjective in character, have relative ends,
the categorical imperative, being objective in character, must have
an absolute end—something whose existence in itself may have
"absolute worth." Then, with a sudden change of tone, he declares:

> Now, I say, man and, in general, every rational being exists as an end
> in himself and not merely as a means to be arbitrarily used by this or
> that will. . . . Beings whose existence does not depend on our will but
> on nature, if they are not rational beings, have only relative worth as
> means, and are therefore called "things"; rational beings, on the other
> hand, are designated "persons" because their nature indicates that they
> are ends in themselves (i.e., things which may not be used merely as
> means). Such a being is thus an object of respect, and as such restricts
> all [arbitrary] choice.[30]

From here, the second formulation of the categorical imperative: *Act
so that you treat humanity, whether in your own person or in that of
another, always as an end and never as a means only.*[31]

What should one say about this further—and allegedly attendant—
role attributed to reason? Even if we accept for the sake of argument,
first, that reason is an all-or-nothing capacity, and second, that nonrational beings are wholly subjected to the laws of causality, a difficulty is immediately evident. As Kenneth Goodpaster remarks:

"End-in-itself" may be the opposite of "End-for-someone" or the opposite of "Means (for someone)." In the argument: "moral judgment
requires that there exist an End-in-itself; all and only rational beings
exist as ends-in-themselves, not as mere means; therefore, all and only
rational beings deserve respect in terms of the requirements of moral
judgment" this ambiguity appears to be a source of invalidity.[32]

In other words: if in the end-in-itself one stresses the *in itself,* that is,
the aspect of universal validity, we are on the side of the first formula
of the categorical imperative; if, alternatively, in the end-in-itself one
stresses the *end,* that is, the aspect of noninstrumentality, we are on
the side of the second formula, and of the things-persons doctrine.
The two formulas are wholly independent, and the apparent derivation of the second from the first is made possible only by the shift in
meaning of the intermediate term.

Many authors express perplexities over both the possible justification and the logical status of the principle that rational nature exists
as an end in itself. While David Ross emphasizes Kant's "great obscurity of expression"[33] in stating it, others maintain that no actual argument is put forward in its defense. After stating the principle, Kant
presents an alleged proof of its validity, which can be summarized as
follows: (a) "man" necessarily thinks of his own existence as an end-in-
itself; (b) every other rational being thinks of his existence in the same
way; (c) as a consequence, it is an objective principle that rational
nature exists as an end-in-itself. Now, there are two possible interpretations of this argument. The first is that (a) and (b) are descriptive
statements; in this case the step to (c), which is a normative statement, is unwarranted. The second is that (a) and (b) are normative
statements, in the sense that they refer to what rationality imposes as
duty (an interpretation that seems to be favored by Kant's reference
to a rational ground underlying all self-evaluations made by rational
beings); in this case, the argument, far from offering a demonstration,
becomes circular. Both interpretations, therefore, lead to a collapse of
the alleged proof.

This is not the only problem. According to Kant's intentions, the
principle that rational nature exists as an end in itself should establish not only a sufficient condition for admission into the moral community (not accidentally called the "realm of ends"), but also a necessary condition. But this is far from following from the proof he
offers. Consider an analogous proof suggested by Christina Hoff: the
human being necessarily thinks of her/his body as extended; every

other corporeal rational being thinks of her/his body in the same way; as a consequence, it is an objective principle that corporeal rational beings have extended bodies. Just as this argument, whatever its soundness, cannot demonstrate that *only* the bodies of corporeal rational beings are extended, so the Kantian argument cannot demonstrate that *only* rational beings are ends-in-themselves.[34]

One last thing is worth considering with regard to the concept of end-in-itself. I have already suggested that sometimes the notion of intrinsic value does not quite replace but rather backs up criteria rooted in subjectivity. This is the case with the Kantian doctrine of absolute worth, in which rationality confers on the being that possesses it not only a particular kind of subjectivity but also a sort of objective value of which subjectivity is just the guardian and maidservant. An example will make this clear. Kant upholds the absolute prohibition of suicide.[35] Such a prohibition falls within the duties toward oneself. But when, let us say, a fully competent individual comes to consider her life so dreadful as to opt for suicide, how is it possible to claim that this choice is precluded just by her duties toward herself? While in a religious context the prohibition can be related to the idea that the individual does not belong to herself but belongs to God, it is hard to find a justification in a secular context. It is here that intrinsic value comes into play. If the very existence of something, in this case rationality, is good in itself, then such a thing is to be preserved irrespective of the inclinations of the subjectivity that might be its bearer: we cannot, Kant states, *under any condition* destroy the rational being—"man"— in our own persons. It is hardly surprising, in the light of this, that the thesis of the intrinsic value of rational beings tends to be seen as a rather controversial aspect of Kant's doctrine even by those authors who accept the humanistic paradigm.

Will and Nature

On the whole, then, it seems that Kant's transition from the first formula, which does not make reference to the moral community, to the second formula, which defines moral patients, is not sound. One has the feeling that the meeting between the notion of end, with the attendant and antithetical notion of means, and the notions of a categorical imperative and a purely formal law is attained only at the cost of a series of shifts in meaning.

The first is the ambiguity between end-in-itself as a universally valid end and end-in-itself as nonmeans. A second appears instead to be connected with the move from (a), the relative value of subjective ends, to (b), the relative value of beings devoid of reason. Such a slip from (a), conditionality of the objects of inclinations, to (b), conditionality (that is, instrumentality) of nonrational beings, is evident if one considers the context of the formulation of the things-persons doctrine. Just before stating it, Kant writes:

> All objects of inclination have only conditional worth . . . The inclinations themselves as the sources of needs, however, are so lacking in absolute worth that the universal wish of every rational being must be indeed to free himself completely from them. Therefore, the worth of any objects to be obtained by our actions is at times conditional.[36]

Immediately following, we find the passage quoted above:

> Beings whose existence does not depend on our will but on nature, if they are not rational beings, have only relative worth as means, and are therefore called "things"; rational beings, on the other hand, are designated "persons" because their nature indicates that they are ends in themselves (i.e., things which may not be used merely as means). Such a being is thus an object of respect, and as such restricts all [arbitrary] choice.[37]

One cannot fail to notice here a patent nonsequitur. Suddenly introducing the "beings whose existence does not depend on our will but on nature," Kant uses in fact the will/nature dichotomy to shift surreptitiously from the opposition between objects of reason and objects of inclination to the quite different opposition between rational beings and nonrational beings.

Is there any possibility of granting the latter opposition an independent foundation? Going on with the discussion of the ends/means doctrine, Kant puts forward a proposal: it is the autonomy of rational beings that makes them the only ends in themselves, thus causing the complete coincidence between the set of moral agents and the set of moral patients.

> [T]he will of a rational being must always be regarded as legislative, for otherwise it could not be thought of as an end in itself. Reason, therefore, relates every maxim of the will as giving universal laws to every other will and also to every action towards itself . . . from the idea of the dignity of a rational being who obeys no law except one which he himself also gives.[38]

What is the argument in this passage? The underlying idea seems to be that rational beings are the existence condition of morality. If one temporarily sets aside the notion of virtuous agent, this is acceptable. But as we emphasized when discussing moral status, one thing is the *how,* that is, the possibility of morality, and another is the *what,* that is, the object of morality. Once again, Kant is making a shift: to respect the autonomy of moral agents in order to maintain the existence conditions of morality does not imply bestowing on moral agents a particular dignity, such as to make them the only moral patients. While respect for moral autonomy, where such autonomy exists, is a truly formal condition, the bestowal of a special dignity is a substantive move. What authorizes this move? Asking this question is tantamount to asking why the principle of universalizability which lies at the heart of morality was confined by Kant only to some of the beings to which the role-shift test can be applied, excluding all nonrational subjectivities. The principle of universalizability directly led one of the most influential contemporary moral philosophers, Richard Hare, to take into consideration the interests of all conscious beings.[39] Why is the result so different in Kant?

Rationality and Humanity

The key to the problem lies, I believe, in the interpretation of the concept of "universal law." Kant holds that the general canon for moral judgment is that "we must be able to will that a maxim of our action become a universal law."[40] This, he argues, can be verified in two ways: (a) some actions are such that their maxim cannot be conceived as a universal law of nature without contradiction, as is the case with false promising (if no one kept their promises, then it would make no sense to promise); and (b) other actions do not imply this inner impossibility, but it is impossible to will that their maxim should be raised to the universality of a law of nature because the will would contradict itself, as is the case with assistance to those in need (one cannot will that a principle of not assisting others in distress prevail because one would find oneself without assistance in case one needed it). And, according to Kant, either of these universalizability tests, though for dissimilar reasons, excludes nonrational beings from moral considerability. We shall therefore consider the tests in turn.

In the first place, what about (a), that is, about the question of the internal impossibility of particular actions? Such a question obviously plays a prominent role within Kant's theory—a role confirmed by the fact that the inner impossibility is related to the sphere of necessary or obligatory duties, while the contradiction of the will is connected only with meritorious or contingent duties. Onora O'Neill, an outstanding contemporary scholar of Kant, remarks that the duties that come under (a) and that include, in addition to refraining from false promising, such fundamental obligations as refraining from coercion and from violence toward others, correspond to negative rights (liberty rights) and can thus be met for *anyone*.[41] What then is the reason why they must not be met for *all* (conscious beings)? True, the institution of promising is in force only among rational beings, and thus the adoption as a universal law of the maxim of not making false promises is self-contradictory only within the realm of rational beings. But this is merely a problem of relevance, concerning one case among many. Interpreting in its light the sphere of application of all other fundamental obligations is tantamount to claiming, for example, that since the right to free speech cannot be sensibly attributed to beings lacking language, then such beings can have no rights at all. For what has the possible effect of universalizing false promising to do with the possible effect of universalizing coercion and violence toward others? What authorizes the slip from a formal determination of ethical principles on the basis of limitations imposed on principles chosen by rational agents, again, as O'Neill puts it[42], to a substantive confinement of the application of such principles to rational agents?

In a revealing passage, Kant himself suggests an answer to this question. While discussing will as a law-giver, he clearly asserts that duty "rests solely on the relation of rational beings to one another."[43] Behind the abstract idea that some actions are such that their maxim cannot be conceived as a universal law of nature without contradiction, there appears therefore the requirement of *reciprocity*. Such requirement lies, as is well known, at the heart of traditional theories of contract, according to which moral norms are the norms with which rational and *self-interested* individuals would agree to comply on condition that others undertook to do so as well. In such a context, one's own compliance is the fair price each one pays to secure others' compliance.

At first sight, the presence of the idea of reciprocity in Kant's theory is not surprising: many authors actually regard the philosopher from Königsberg as the forerunner of certain sorts of contractarian doctrines, chief among them John Rawls's theory of justice. Nonetheless, something seems to have gone wrong. What has a conceptual reference to self-interest (however implicit) to do with a theory that denies a role even to benevolent inclinations? Is it possible that behind the Kantian agent-patient parity principle one may after all discover what we have called the silver rule—"treat others as they would treat you"? The thesis is not implausible. It has already been put forward by Schopenhauer, who in *On the Basis of Morality* does not hesitate to claim that in Kant's theory "moral obligation rests absolutely and entirely on assumed *reciprocity*. Consequently, it is utterly egoistic and obtains its interpretation from egoism. Under the condition of *reciprocity*, egoism cunningly acquiesces in a compromise."[44]. But if things are like this, it is obvious that, in the case of universal laws that fall under (a), nonrational beings can be excluded only at the price of a deep, though concealed, inconsistency within the Kantian system.

Although different, the difficulties by which an exclusive interpretation of (b), that is, of the test of the contradiction of the will, is beset are even more apparent. Edward Johnson summarizes:

> Kant presumably wants to hold that even someone whom, as it turns out, is never in distress cannot *will* this maxim. For the question is what one judges for the hypothetical situation in which one needs help: one must, on Kant's view, judge that one wants to be helped in such a case. But there is no requirement that one be, in this hypothetical situation, a rational creature. One must be rational, to be sure, in order to make the judgment, in order to *will* anything. But one judges on the basis of one's interests in various (hypothetical) situations in which one need not be rational. Maxims or principles that are "universally valid as a law for every subject" can only be willed by rational beings, but they need not . . . restrict respect to rational beings.[45]

Somehow, thus, it seems that we have come back to the golden rule—more precisely, to its formulation in positive terms: Do unto others as you would have them do unto you. This leads one to hold that, contra Kant, it is arbitrary in the case of (b) to exclude from what is essentially the role-shift test the beings that, though lacking reason, are nonetheless conscious.

It seems, then, that Kant's exclusive stance can be supported neither by version (a) nor by version (b) of the universalizability test—not by the former because the exclusive interpretation would contradict the general foundations of the doctrine in which it is included, and not by the latter because such interpretation would require an arbitrary application of the test. If this is so, even the last defense of such a stance collapses, and, as a consequence, the overall answer to the question from which we started is negative: despite its complexity, the Kantian version of the criterion of rationality cannot meet the burden of proof imposed by the test of contextual relevance. Kant, in other words, did not succeed in his endeavor to confine the sphere of application of the categorical imperative, and the moral protection ensuing from it, to rational beings alone.

Still less, therefore, did he succeed in the endeavor to *establish* humanism—he only *created* it, if not from nothing then at least from foundations that are not able to support it. For if the criterion of rationality proves to be without valid justification, the position of the criterion of membership in the human species is even shakier. In the first place, Kant does not ascribe species membership moral relevance of a direct kind but only of a derivative one. It is the possession of reason that grants one the status of moral patient, and humans are moral patients in so far as they are rational beings. As a consequence, every difficulty met with by the criterion of rationality rebounds upon the criterion of species membership. Second, once the metaphysical components of the theory are given up, it is evident that from an empirical point of view the category of rational beings is not coextensive with the category of human beings. On the contrary, according to the level of rationality requested, one might exclude some humans or include some nonhumans. As a result, the Kantian version of human equality is doubly untenable.

In the face of this tangle of difficulties, nothing sounds simpler than the reply made to Kant at the beginning of the twentieth century by Leonard Nelson, a German philosopher belonging to his school. Here Nelson refers to nonhumans, but his argument could hold equally good for human beings lacking reason:

> If we apply the criterion of duty, the question of whether animals have rights can be readily answered: we have merely to ask whether, in considering an action affecting an animal, we could assent to such an action after abstracting from numerical determination. *In other words, we have to ask whether we would consent to be used as mere means by another being far superior to us in strength and intelligence.* This question answers itself. The fact that man has other beings in his power, and that he is in a position to use them as means to his own ends, is purely fortuitous.[46]

In contrasting the idea of reciprocity with the idea of assent, Nelson not only anticipates some aspects of the most recent reflection within contractarian theory but also makes clear to which conclusions the Kantian version of universalizability would lead us if impartially considered.

Ethics Makes a Turn: Utilitarianism

Perhaps as a result of both the chronological priority and the theoretical prevalence of virtue ethics, for a great deal of its history Western moral philosophy has given center stage to moral agents. All the authors examined up until now, from Aristotle to Thomas Aquinas to Descartes to Kant, have defended some version of the agent-patient parity principle. At the same time Kant was giving this approach its paradigmatic form, however, a doctrine arose in England that would bring about a radical change in perspective:

> Nature has placed mankind under the governance of two sovereign masters, *pain* and *pleasure*. It is for them alone to point out what we ought to do, as well as to determine what we shall do. . . . The *principle of utility* recognises this subjection, and assumes it for the foundation of that system, the object of which is to rear the fabric of felicity by the hands of reason and law. Systems which attempt to question it, deal in sounds instead of sense, in caprice instead of reason, in darkness instead of light.[47]

This is the striking opening of the *Principles of Morals and Legislation* by Jeremy Bentham, and at the same time the start of a school of ethics that, thoroughly abandoning any connection with religion and tradition, was to deeply influence two centuries of moral and political philosophy.

Actually, Bentham is not the only author to which this revolution is to be ascribed. By his own admission, it is to David Hume that the first formulation of the system that sees in utility the test and measure of every action and behavior—as well as, one might add, the modern idea of an ethics that does not need God[48]—is owed. Nonetheless, the organic and detailed formulation that turned this system into a serious competitor of the approach until then predominant, and later on of Kantianism, was supplied by Bentham.

Normative ethics has to do with principles concerning *the right* and *the good*. Within it, therefore, one can find theories focusing on either of the two notions. Currently, two theoretical families, the deontological and the consequentialist, dominate the field of moral philosophy. Deontological theories take the notion of right as fundamental and defend the obligatoriness/nonobligatoriness of actions in themselves: an action can/should be right independently of its consequences. Consequentialist theories, on the other hand, focus on the good, usually interpreted in a nonmoral sense: actions are to be judged on the basis of their consequences in terms of the production of better or worse states of affairs.

Kantianism obviously falls within the former sphere; Benthamite utilitarianism is the example par excellence of the latter. More specifically, Bentham asserts that there is only one ultimate moral principle, the principle of utility, which states that when confronted with a choice between different actions or social policies, we must opt for the alternative that produces the best consequences for everyone affected. Although utilitarianism has historically been subject to continuous refinements and transformations, some of which we will meet with later on, it is worthwhile to concentrate first on its classic formulation, with the aim of becoming aware not only of its general novelty but also of its radical implications for the question of moral status.

Bentham and the End of the Agent-Patient Parity Principle

In quantitative terms, Bentham devotes little space to nonhumans, but his few sentences on the subject are fundamental. It is to a note of the *Principles* that the Australian philosopher Peter Singer made reference when he reopened the debate on the ethical treatment of animals. The passage is now well known but is worth quoting in detail. Bentham is considering what are the beings which on the one hand can be affected by the actions of the agent and on the other are susceptible of happiness. He identifies two categories: (a) other human beings, and (b) other animals, who, he adds, on account of the insensibility of the ancient jurists, were degraded into the class of things. At this point he inserts the note in question:

> Why have [the interests of the rest of the animal creation] not, universally, [met] with as much [attention] as those of human creatures, allowance made for the difference in point of sensibility? Because the laws that are have been the work of mutual fear; a sentiment which the less rational animals have not had the same means as man has of turning to account. Why *ought* they not? No reason can be given. . . .

The day *may* come, when the rest of the animal creation may acquire those rights which never could have been withholden from them but by the hand of tyranny. The French have already discovered that the blackness of the skin is no reason why a human being should be abandoned without redress to the caprice of a tormentor. It may come one day to be recognized, that the number of the legs, the villosity of the skin, or the termination of the *os sacrum,* are reasons equally insufficient for abandoning a sensitive being to the same fate. What else is it that should trace the insuperable line? Is it the faculty of reason, or, perhaps, the faculty of discourse? But a full-grown horse or dog is beyond comparison a more rational, as well as a more conversable animal, than an infant of a day, or a week, or even a month, old. But suppose the case were otherwise, what would it avail? the question is not, Can they *reason?* nor, Can they *talk?* but, Can they *suffer?*[49]

It is difficult to imagine something farther from Cartesian and Kantian abstractions. The actual exclusion of nonhumans from the moral community is explained not on the grounds of an alleged lack of intrinsic value but by making reference to mere power relations. The subjection of beings traditionally categorized as no more than things is compared to the subjection of many members of our own species. With the vanishing of any unbridgeable metaphysical gulf connected with linguistic ability or reason, the "other animals" become again the conscious and sensitive beings they always have been for common sense, while, through the reference to the direct duty to take their interests into consideration, Bentham grants them the status of moral patients. What made such a change possible?

The principle on which classical utilitarianism is founded is, in Bentham's words as well as in subsequent formulations, the principle of the "greatest happiness." While within this phrase the highlighted element is often that of maximization, it is in the prominence of the notion of happiness that the key to the expansion of the moral community lies. For if, as we have noticed, the question from which Western philosophy usually started was, "what are the existence conditions of morality?" and this caused the answers to be developed as from a theory of the agent, Bentham proceeds in the opposition direction. For him, the fundamental problem is the question, "what is the object of morality?" and this has the effect of shifting attention on to the entities that can be morally taken into consideration.

At the center of ethics, then, there are moral patients—concrete individuals who are empirically characterized by the inclination to avoid pain and to pursue happiness. The obligations of agents stem from such a way of being of patients. The duty of moral agents is not to implement abstract rules in their dealings with other agents but rather to produce the greatest favorable balance of happiness over pain for all beings affected by their actions. The effects of the shift in perspective are particularly clear at the end of the note quoted. Against the characteristics traditionally appealed to as requisites for moral agency, and then surreptitiously turned into requisites for moral patiency, Bentham sets a criterion arising out of the direct consideration of what it means to be a patient: the capacity for being harmed or benefited, and therefore, at the very least, the possession of interests—in our terms, consciousness.

In his comment on Bentham's passage, Peter Singer clearly illustrates the justification of the criterion of the capacity for suffering for inclusion in the moral community:

> The capacity for suffering—or more strictly, for suffering and/or enjoyment or happiness—is not just another characteristic like the capacity for language or higher mathematics. Bentham is not saying that those who try to mark "the insuperable line" that determines whether the interests of a being should be considered happen to have chosen the wrong characteristic. . . . The capacity for suffering and enjoyment is *a prerequisite for having interests at all,* a condition that must be satisfied before we can speak of interests in a meaningful way. It would be nonsense to say that it was not in the interests of a stone to be kicked along the road by a schoolboy. A stone does not have interests because it cannot suffer. Nothing that we can do to it could possibly make any difference to its welfare. The capacity for suffering and enjoyment is, however, not only necessary, but also sufficient for us to say that a being has interests—at an absolute minimum, an interest in not suffering. A mouse, for example, does have an interest in not being kicked along the road, because it [*sic*] will suffer if it is.[50]

Of course, Bentham's theory faces a number of challenges. Among them, two at least need to be briefly considered here because of their direct relation with the extension of the moral community. The first concerns motivation. While failing to offer any proof of the principle of utility, and indeed maintaining that "that which is used to prove every thing else, cannot itself be proved,"[51] Bentham in fact makes very exacting demands on moral agents. The obligation always to act in view of the best consequences for all beings affected not only imposes a notable burden but also requires an extremely strong motivation, which is not easy to offer. Bentham puts forward two solutions for this difficulty. One is the reference, once again along Hume's lines, to the "purely social motive of sympathy or benevolence,"[52] which is supposed to be present in moral agents—and, in this case, the impression of inadequate effectiveness is not dispelled. The other, however, is more interesting. It lies in the inclusion in the felicific system of pain and pleasure not only as final causes but also as efficient causes, that is, as sanctions.[53] Sanctions have the task of making the greatest happiness of each one coincide with the greatest happiness of others. Through reward (positive sanction) and punishment (negative sanction) the agent is driven to increase or diminish her happiness in unison with others' happiness. Although Bentham examines different kinds of sanctions, a fundamental role is played by the one he defines as *political,* that is, by the sanction dispensed by the legal system. We will have occasion to go back to the significance of this institutional aspect.

The second problem concerns the calculation of interests. How is it possible, one might ask, to weigh and, above all, to compare the huge quantity and variety of the pleasures and pains of the beings included in the moral community? Bentham's solution is simple and clear. What is needed is a "hedonic calculus," on the basis of which pleasures and pains—after being carefully listed and classified—can be measured according to seven fundamental parameters: intensity, duration, certainty, propinquity, fecundity, purity, and extent. With this proposal Bentham, while letting hardly negligible practical difficulties persist, overcomes an important theoretical difficulty. For it is manifest that his list excludes any qualitative evaluations, and that the confinement to quantitative parameters makes at least abstractly possible the sort of universal comparison that the doctrine requires. Once again, this conflicts with the approach prevailing as from Aristotle, which arranged mental experiences along a hierarchical/ qualitative scale culminating in the aspects connected with rationality. But Bentham does not flinch: "Quantity of pleasure being equal, pushpin is as good as poetry."

It is important to quite understand the meaning of this well known aphorism. Having renounced any metaphysical pretension, and therefore any attribution of value founded upon specific worldviews, classical utilitarianism entrusts axiology to subjectivity. This is the basis of Bentham's rigorous egalitarianism: every interest counts as much as it weighs for its particular bearer, whatever its specific content. Of course, this holds as well in the case of nonhumans capable of experiencing pain or pleasure.

An Uncompleted Transformation

By means of the criterion of the possession of interests, utilitarianism has introduced the other animals into the moral community. But can one say it has also granted them a status comparable to that of human beings? Such a question, which concerns comparative levels, is somewhat complicated, and, in order to deal with it, it may be useful to push our gaze beyond Bentham. In a rejoinder to the Kantian philosopher William Whewell, who had claimed that the tie of human brotherhood binds us to increase human pleasure not only because it is pleasure but because it is *human* pleasure, John Stuart Mill actually lets the attitude toward nonhumans be a test of the utilitarian doctrine:

> According to the standard of Dr. Whewell the slavemasters and the nobles were right. They too felt themselves "bound" by a "tie of brotherhood" to the white men and to the nobility . . . We are perfectly willing to stake the whole question on this one issue. Granted that any practice causes more pain to animals than it gives pleasures to man [*sic*]; is that practice moral or immoral? And if, exactly in proportion as human beings raise their heads out of the slough of selfishness, they do not with one voice answer "immoral," let the morality of the principle of utility be for ever condemned.[54]

Though less emphatic, Henry Sidgwick's position is along the same lines. To the question of who the "all" are whose happiness is to be taken into account, after remarking that Bentham and Mill had opted for the inclusion of animals, he replies that such extensionistic approach is indeed the one most in accordance with the universality that is characteristic of the principle of utility. [55]

The idea that nonhumans are included among moral patients thus runs like a thread through classical utilitarianism. But, as Edward Johnson acutely remarked, the whole utilitarian tradition is based on assertion and qualification.[56] The other animals are in principle included on a par in the felicific calculus; afterward, however, their ethical treatment is somehow differentiated from that of humans, with concrete implications that often do not much deviate from the status quo. Just before comparing human and nonhuman slavery, Bentham surprisingly writes with regard to animals:

> If the being eaten were all, there is very good reason why we should be suffered to eat such of them as we like to eat: we are the better for it, and they are never the worse. They have none of those long-protracted

anticipations of future misery which we have. The death they suffer in our hands commonly is, and always may be, a speedier and by that means a less painful one, than that which would await them in the inevitable course of nature. . . . But is there any reason why we should be suffered to torment them? Not any that I can see.[57]

Bentham here falls below his normal standard of argument.[58] In the first place, even according to knowledge available at the end of the eighteenth century, it was evident that nonhumans driven to the abattoir had an inkling of what awaited them and showed panic. Second, killing for food is not, and has never been, painless—on the contrary, it is, and was perhaps to a greater degree in the past, a procedure implying severe suffering. The empirical assumptions appealed to in this context are patently false.

Nonetheless, Bentham does offer an argument: he singles out the inability to "anticipate future misery" as the morally relevant characteristic allowing one to draw a line between humans and nonhumans. The note he strikes is important, for the capacity to have a sense of future is often considered as crucial in the contemporary debate on the value of life. But whatever its plausibility, the argument—to which we shall return—is here applied in an arbitrary manner. It is in fact undeniable that there exist human beings—many intellectually disabled people, for example—who have scarce, if any, sense of future. Why, therefore, confine the argument to nonhumans?

Finally, there is an internal objection. On the perspective of hedonistic utilitarianism, what counts is the total quantity of pain and pleasure. The harm that killing causes, therefore, has to do not only with the possible fear of death but also with the elimination of the possible future happiness of the being involved. If such being is healthy and has no particular problems, then one can suppose that the taking of its life detracts from its happiness, irrespective of its capacity for anticipation; and such detraction of happiness can even acquire in the hedonic calculus a greater negative weight than the "anticipations of future misery." As a consequence, Bentham cannot but at the price of theoretical inconsistency make beings lacking a sense of future a distinct category as far as death is concerned.

Overall, it seems that what lurks behind these lines is once again the classical—although not always appropriate to utilitarianism—distinction between benevolence and justice. The injunction against tormenting is usually tied to benevolence, that is, to the secondary family of moral ideas turning on notions like compassion and charity, while the prohibition on taking life tends to be connected to the higher ethical sphere of justice. Indeed, the hidden presence of this distinction is inadvertently confirmed by Sidgwick when, without advancing any justification, he mentions duties toward nonhumans only within the context of the discussion of benevolence and confines himself to replacing the Benthamite injunction against tormenting them with the duty not to cause them "unnecessary pain."[59]

If, therefore, both Bentham and Sidgwick arbitrarily assign second-class moral status to nonhumans, what about Mill? Despite his alleged willingness to stake the whole "morality of the principle of utility" on the issue of nonhumans, not even Mill breaks with the utilitarian tradition of assertion and qualification. Insofar as the interests of other animals are analogous to human interests, they are owed equal consideration. Nevertheless, nonhuman interests *are not always* analogous to human interests. And this is because, he claims, it is "better to be a human being dissatisfied than a pig satisfied."[60]

What is one to make of this statement? Apparently, Mill assumes that pleasures that are (alleged to be) specifically human—intellectual pleasures, for example—deserve greater weight in the utilitarian calculus than the pleasures (alleged to be) characteristic of nonhumans—bodily pleasures, for example. It is not difficult to realize that this marks a major deviation from Benthamite theory. While Bentham may underestimate empirical data about the capacities of humans and nonhumans, he never deviates from the idea that the appraisal of pain and pleasure must be merely quantitative. The quantitative approach is a fundamental aspect of Benthamism. Mill's distinction between superior and inferior pleasures breaks this homogeneity, introducing two new complications: that of the establishment of the two levels and that of the weighting of qualitatively different elements.

The latter problem seems to go unanswered, since Mill remarks that, in comparison with qualitative superiority, the quantitative dimension of the inferior pleasure becomes "of small account"—which somehow implies acceptance of incommensurability and hence results in making a hedonic calculus in the Benthamite style impossible. As for the former complication, Mill does put forward a suggestion: the recourse to the method of the "competent judge." "Of two pleasures," he says, "if there be one to which all or almost all who have experience of both give a decided preference . . . that is the more desirable pleasure."[61] With some variations, such method is still employed in the ethical debate, and later on we will consider its most recent version.

As regards Mill's suggestion, however, it has been aptly observed that the introduction of the restrictive clause "or *almost* all" gives rise to difficulties. For what about those who prefer the lower pleasures? Should we consider them incompetent judges? Or should their position lead one to revise the more general judgment?[62]

These difficulties, which stem from Mill's attempt to remain on the level of subjectivity, point at a more fundamental question: Can the general opinion take on the role once played by the alleged objectivity of specific worldviews? In other words: Where the guarantee of a judgment's soundness cannot any longer come either from God or from metaphysics, can the mere force of numbers override the judgment of the individual? The case of the dissenting judges does nothing but bring to light the implausibility of this suggestion. If three individuals distinct from myself cannot have their judgment prevail over mine, why should one thousand, or one hundred thousand be able to do so? It is clear that the appeal to the competent judge cannot play the role that Mill wants to bestow on it. As a consequence, just like the problem of the comparison between qualitatively different elements, the problem of the establishment of the two levels remains unsolved in the end, and Mill's account does not turn out to be able to justify the alleged disanalogy between the interests that are (assumed to be) distinctive of humans and the interests that are (assumed to be) distinctive of nonhumans.

After the Inclusion

In the light of all this, one can conclude that classical utilitarianism did not tackle the problem of the comparative status of humans and nonhumans in a theoretically satisfactory way. And, after Sidgwick, for about a century moral philosophy would lose any interest in the matter. While the continental tradition, with the exception of Leonard Nelson, limited itself to uncritically reiterating the indirect duties view, Great Britain saw the gradual establishment of the Hegelian school, assuredly not very prone to be concerned with nonhumans. As for the specifically utilitarian strand, the influence of G. E. Moore's "ideal" version, where pain and pleasure give way to much more abstract values such as aesthetic experience and interpersonal relationships, gradually made the topics central to English philosophical radicalism, and therefore the animal question, disappear from the scene.[63] To Moore's views we somehow also owe the start of the long period dominated by the interest in metaethics, during which most substantive problems were simply abandoned.

The revival takes place with the (re)birth of applied ethics. At the beginning of the 1970s, Peter Singer resumes the classical utilitarian discussion where it had been interrupted, developing for the first time in a consistent way the principle that like interests should be accorded like consideration. Shortly afterward, assumptions previously taken for granted come to be challenged within other ethical approaches as well, and in particular within rights theory, traditionally linked to the agent-patient parity principle. In brief, what is called into question is the idea that animals are second-class moral patients and hence the kinds of beings that can be treated in ways we would deem it impermissible to treat human beings. And, irrespective of the different normative proposals put forward, the arguments underlying the critical phase are shared by all the views in question. It is to these arguments that we shall now turn.

Chapter 4

■■■

Speciesism

While discussing the criteria of moral status in the second chapter, we provisionally set aside the appeal to membership in the species *Homo sapiens*. Because of some peculiarities, such a criterion will be treated as a separate case. In the first place, owing to its simplicity, it is extremely powerful and widespread at the social level. Second, on a more theoretical plane, it can be found not only by itself but in combination with other criteria as well. As a result of this, its necessary justifications are not always put forward. Finally, as we already know, this criterion has recently been brought to the fore again by the recasting in secular terms of the sanctity-of-life doctrine.

In addition, it is worth noting that, after being a criterion for inclusion in the moral community, the criterion of species membership was transformed into a comparative criterion for having special moral status. It is thus possible to use it as a bridge-element in order to shift from the question of basic moral status, which we tackled defending the criterion of consciousness, to the question of possible levels within the moral community, which will concern us henceforth.

According to the current moral paradigm, all human beings are equal and are entitled to the same fundamental moral protection. Animals, on the other hand, while counting for something, have an utterly inferior status: the protection granted to them is minimal, usually lying only in the prohibition of wanton cruelty. Species membership determines inclusion in either of the two moral categories.

Humanism—as this intrahuman egalitarian approach was defined—has therefore two sides: an inclusive side, according to which *all* humans are first-class moral patients, and an exclusive side, according to which *only* humans are first-class moral patients. Alan Gewirth—a philosopher to whose important attempt to provide a logical justification for adhesion to the golden rule we will later return—writes that all basic moral rights are human and that "for human rights to be had, one must only be human."[1] And in a paper presented at the Oxford Amnesty Lectures of 1993, after deploring the difficult socioeconomic conditions under which the majority of men and women on the planet still live, Richard Rorty regretfully points out that this makes them simply unable to understand why membership in a biological species is supposed to suffice for membership in a moral community.[2]

For some time now, understanding why species membership is ipso facto moral membership has been difficult for many moral philosophers as well. Of course, what Rorty is concerned with here is the inclusive aspect of humanism—he adds, in fact, that the human beings he is referring to "live in a world in which it would be just too risky . . . to let one's sense of moral community stretch beyond one's family, clan or tribe."[3] What the moral philosophers involved question is instead the exclusive aspect of the humanistic doctrine. And "speciesism" is the term they currently employ to refer to the idea that humans qua humans have a privileged moral status compared to any other conscious beings.

The notion of speciesism could actually be used to describe any form of discrimination based on species. However, the line we have drawn between members of *Homo sapiens* and all other animals is so salient from the moral point of view that the concept has come to be seen as practically interchangeable with the notion of human chauvinism. It is therefore in this specific sense that I will employ it from now on. The term speciesism was coined on the model of racism and sexism. The neologism thus alludes to the intrahuman prejudices that contemporary egalitarianism condemns. The first, fundamental objection that Peter Singer raises is based just on this parallel.

Although the quotation of Bentham's statement, "The question is not, Can they *reason?* nor, Can they *talk?* but, Can they *suffer?*" with its reference to the possession of interests as the only morally relevant characteristic, also indicates an alternative criterion, at the core of Singer's criticism lies an *ad hominem* argument—that is, a charge of inconsistency directed at the egalitarian paradigm. In short, the idea is that it is not possible to deny a moral role to race or sex membership while at the same time attributing a moral role to species.

> Racists violate the principle of equality by giving greater weight to the interests of members of their own race when there is a clash between their interests and the interests of those of another race. Sexists violate the principle of equality by favoring the interests of their own sex. Similarly, speciesists allow the interests of their own species to override the greater interests of members of other species. The pattern is identical in each case.[4]

The consequence of this is that ethical positions which, while rejecting sexism and racism, accept speciesism are internally inconsistent.

Such a charge must be taken seriously. Even if it turned out, as some maintain, that in ethics it is not possible to offer objectively valid justifications, it is still possible to address to moral positions or systems objectively valid criticisms.[5] One among these is the charge of inconsistency: if particular principles or judgments are contradictorily applied, the overall position is untenable. Today we can easily understand how unsatisfactory the egalitarian attitude of those who fought for the so-called "universal suffrage" yet limited its attribution to male human beings actually was. A like situation occurs when contemporary moral egalitarianism is confined to the members of the species *Homo sapiens*.

Nonetheless, however serious, this objection does not reach the heart of the problem, but merely pushes it backward. Though the support of a long tradition grants speciesism an air of respectability that (at least today) analogous intrahuman discriminations lack, a rejoinder can still be put forward: even in case one acknowledges that speciesism is comparable to racism and sexism, this still doesn't prove that speciesism is wrong—not, at least, until it is shown that racism and sexism are wrong.

Traditional Speciesism: Attributing Weight to Biological Characteristics

The question to be addressed is, then, why neither race nor sex nor species membership should play a role when it comes to deciding how individuals should be treated.

As far as race and sex are concerned, liberal political philosophy tends to appeal to the Rawlsian idea of "natural lottery." David Richards, for example, claims that "fortuitous" facts about the physical characteristics or social background of human beings are irrelevant "by definition" to the moral point of view, since morality involves treating individuals as individuals, apart from class or color, clan or caste, talent or nationality: "Since these differences between persons are fortuitous, they cannot be of fundamental weight in deciding what count as moral principles."[6]

This answer suffers from circularity. Once it is made explicit, Richards's argument is this: some facts about individuals—fortuitous facts—are morally irrelevant because morality involves treating individuals irrespective of these facts, insofar as they are fortuitous. It is clear that fortuitousness is for Richards a substantive moral notion having to do with prior ideas of fairness. The result is that here the reference to the idea of "irrelevancy," rather than providing an explanation, requires an explanation.[7]

Nonetheless, it is just the notion of relevancy that may indicate another path. It is a point we have already met with, albeit in a different form. In criticizing the notion of ontological status, we pointed out that ethics is an autonomous theoretical inquiry, which not only can be tackled by rational methods but is also endowed with its own standards of justification and criticism. But if ethical questions must be determined through the application of standards internal to the discipline itself, then it seems correct to maintain that criteria imported from other domains cannot be morally relevant *in themselves*.

This obviously holds for science as well. Race and sex are biological classifications. They have to do with skin color or eye shape, with reproductive role or genital structure, or with muscular mass or distribution of hair of the body rather than with the capacity for being harmed or benefited, with interests, desires, virtues or welfare. This determines a priori that they can play no *direct* role in ethics. In other words, their introduction in the context of moral argument, far from offering a justification, stands in need of justification.

It is interesting to note that a view of this kind, though only partially articulated, can be found in common sense. Our great fascination with the idea that there may exist in the universe other intelligent beings with which we could communicate (think of the success of the science fiction character ET) shows that what we regard as important is not having a certain biological pedigree but rather possessing psychological characteristics similar to our own—characteristics that lie at the source of all that matters in our lives.

In the face of all this, it is clear that, failing to meet the prerequisite of moral relevance, the appeal to race or sex membership is unacceptable as a comparative criterion of moral status. The appeal to species membership is therefore equally unacceptable.

The Correspondence Approach: Species as a Mark of the Morally Relevant Characteristics

Against the interpretation of the moral (ir)relevance of membership in a biological group advanced here, an objection can be raised. One might claim, as some critics have done, that empirically there is a correspondence between some biological characteristics and the presence or absence of capacities that are morally relevant, so that biological group membership may be appealed to as a mark of this difference. In this light, the appeal to the biological characteristic would meet, though in an indirect way, the prerequisite of moral relevance. We can call this the "correspondence approach." It is worthwhile to point out that racists have often used this argument, by asserting, for example, that members of other races are less rational, less sensitive, or generally less intellectually gifted than members of their own race. As several egalitarian philosophers have emphasized, the reasons put forward in favor of racial discrimination often seek to connect biological elements with aspects that could have direct moral relevance— in most cases with the possession, or lack, of specific psychological attributes.[8] We know that any such connection tends to be firmly rejected by intrahuman egalitarians. Even if it existed, however, the argument would remain deeply flawed.

To understand why, it is useful to set out a more formal version of the correspondence approach. Put as a syllogism, it would read more or less as follows: psychological characteristics a, b, and c are endowed with particular moral relevance; these characteristics are present to a greater extent in biological group x than in biological group y; therefore, we are morally entitled to afford to every member of group x a treatment different from, and better than, the treatment afforded to every member of group y. Can we say that the conclusion follows from the premises? Yes, but only on condition that a further premise is tacitly assumed, according to which every single member of group x possesses the characteristics in question to a greater degree than every single member of group y.

The problem with the correspondence approach is that, whatever the selected characteristics, what we shall find will be overlappings, not mutual exclusion, between groups. Let us suppose that the members of a particular biological group, A, are typically more intelligent than the members of another biological group, B: there surely will be members of group A less intelligent than the average for their group or members of group B more intelligent than the average for their group. How should we treat such "atypical" individuals?

If, in such a context, we want to retain the reference to the biological characteristic, we should treat them according to their group membership. Thomas Scanlon, for example, stated along these lines that it seems that moral status depends not on a particular being's actual capacities but on the capacities that are typical of its kind.[9] To show how implausible this argument is, it may be useful to refer to a thought experiment suggested by Michael Tooley.[10] Imagine that we grant the right to life on the basis of the possession of rationality, and let John and Mary be two individuals who are not rational beings, and who belong to two different biological groups, but who are indistinguishable with respect to their psychological capacities and their mental lives. John might belong to a group 99 percent of which are rational beings, while Mary might belong to a group of which only 1 percent are rational beings. If we adopt Scanlon's view, it will be wrong to kill John but it will be right to kill Mary. It is also possible to make a less dramatic but more concrete example. Suppose that we discovered that women in general are less gifted than men for particular jobs. Even if this were the case, there would certainly be women more gifted than the average, or at least more gifted than some men. Surely we would not accept in such a case that men endowed with lesser capacities were given preference over these women for jobs requiring the level of capacities they actually have, on the grounds that women and men should be treated according not to their actual characteristics, but to what is typical of their "kind." The blatant irrationality of the view that individuals should be treated not on the basis of their qualities but on the basis of other beings' qualities undermines any plausibility the correspondence approach might have seemed to have.

A more abstract formulation of this conclusion may be offered. This is what James Rachels does through a general view about the justification of judgments concerning how individuals may be treated. According to such a view, which he defines as "moral individualism," the treatment of individuals is to be determined not by their group membership but by their own individual characteristics.[11] In other words, moral individualism can be seen as a formal requirement that is prima facie imposed on ethical theorizing by rationality—a requirement on the basis of which what must be taken into account in the assignment of moral status are the organisms' own attributes, and not the classes to which organisms are ascribed. However simple it may appear, this idea challenges a perspective that has long characterized Western philosophical tradition.

Racism, Sexism, and Speciesism: An Objection to the Parallel

Moral individualism seems to constitute a powerful argument not only against racism and sexism but also against speciesism. Some authors, however, have rejected this conclusion. In particular, they have denied that the criticism of the correspondence approach can hold also in the case of the appeal to membership in the species *Homo sapiens* as a criterion for the attribution of superior moral status. And this is because, it is argued, unlike what happens with race and sex, between our species and the others there is none of those areas of overlap, which, by creating a divergence between the psychological and the biological criterion, make reference to group membership irrational. More specifically, speciesism would be morally defensible because, empirically, the fact of being human allegedly marks, relative to members of other species, a radical difference in the possession of the characteristics deemed to be morally relevant.

A similar idea seems to underlie traditional approaches to political philosophy. Usually, in fact, political philosophers merely take for granted the existence of two separate and quite homogenous spheres, one including all nonhuman animals and the other including instead all human beings, seen as equally endowed with the morally favored characteristics. Following Hume and his account of the circumstances of justice, for example, a strand of thought within contemporary contractarianism keeps inserting *relative equality* among members of our species within the "normal conditions under which human cooperation is both possible and necessary,"[12] to use the words of John Rawls. And in his widely discussed book *Anarchy, State and Utopia,* Robert

Nozick, after maintaining that a being has rights only if it is a free and rational moral agent, endowed with the "ability to regulate and guide its life in accordance with some overall conception it chooses to accept,"[13] grants rights to *all* humans.

Such an approach suffers from excessive abstraction. As we suggested in criticizing the views of Kant and Bentham, concretely it is not true that all human beings possess the attributes that allegedly mark the difference between us and the other animals. It is undeniable that there exist within our species individuals who, on account of structural problems due to genetic or developmental anomalies, or of contingent problems due to diseases or accidents, will never acquire, or have forever lost, the characteristics—autonomy, rationality, self-consciousness, and the like—that we consider as typically human. To resort again to the terminology that we used in criticizing the sanctity-of-life doctrine, there are members of our species—the brain-damaged, the severely intellectually disabled, the anencephalics, the irreversibly comatose, the senile—who, while being human in the biological sense, are not human in the philosophical sense.

The argument advanced here, now known as the "argument from marginal cases," has been formulated in various ways by animal defense theorists.[14] Of its several aspects, one in particular concerns us here. It is the fact that, covering as it does a wide range of intellectual and emotional levels, the presence of these atypical human beings leads, with respect to members of other species, just to that series of overlappings that the advocates of the correspondence approach would wish to deny. This means that not even in the case of species can group membership be used as the mark of a different endowment with respect to the morally favored characteristics. As a consequence, just as with appeals to race and sex, the appeal to species membership cannot play even an indirect role in the definition of levels of moral status. When it comes to determining the treatment of beings, there are no exceptions to moral individualism.

An Attempt to Grant Paradigmatic Status to Nonparadigmatic Humans

The idea that speciesism is an arbitrary discrimination analogous to racism and sexism is not easy to accept within the framework of a philosophical tradition that has always confined nonhumans in a separate moral category. Is there any way to avoid such a conclusion? In the face of the problem of marginal cases, two escape routes have been attempted.

The first one involves trying to deny that there may actually be any overlapping between nonparadigmatic humans and members of species other than our own. This would allow the retrieval of the correspondence approach, and thus of the (indirect) moral relevance of membership in the species *Homo sapiens*. Carl Cohen, a philosopher from the University of Michigan who defends the view that only moral agents can have rights, is perhaps the most representative among the authors who tried this way. In an article defending the choice to use animals, but not human beings, in biomedical experimentation, Cohen admits that there are humans with reduced abilities who lack the capacity for moral agency. Nonetheless, he emphatically rejects the idea that such individuals may be put on the same moral level as nonhumans. This is his argument:

> The capacity for moral judgment that distinguishes humans from animals is not a test to be administered to human beings one by one. Persons [*sic*] who are unable, because of some disability, to perform the full moral functions natural to human beings are certainly not for that reason ejected from the moral community. *The issue is one of kind.* Humans are of such a kind that they may be the subject of experiments only with their voluntary consent. The choices they make freely must be respected. . . . What humans retain when disabled, animals never had.[15]

Apparently, we are here faced with the old argument that beings are to be treated on the basis of what is normal for their kind. And in fact, there are authors who have interpreted Cohen's argument as a mere appeal to group membership and therefore as a reformulation of Scanlon's argument. It seems to me, however, that the last sentence— "What humans retain when disabled, animals never had"—leads in a different direction, and that Cohen's use of the notion of "kind" does not point at statistical considerations about the average of the capacities within a group but rather at a thesis about the *nature* of the beings involved.

On the face of it, the idea that human "nature" radically differs from the nature of other animals is implausible. In 1747, Linnaeus, author of the modern system of classifying plants and animals, wrote to a friend: "I demand of you, and of the whole world, that you show me a generic character . . . by which to distinguish between Man and Ape. I myself most assuredly know of none."[16] Today we can better put into perspective Linnaeus's observation. Midway through the 1980s, molecular biologists divulged the first results of the application of the DNA clock method to human origins, thus making it possible to tackle the problem of our relationships with the beings evolutionarily closest to us. The outcome was that we differ from common chimpanzees and pigmy chimpanzees by about 1.6 percent of DNA, from gorillas by 2.3 percent and from orangutans by 3.6 percent. On the basis of the first of these results, some authors did what Linnaeus had not dared to do, suggesting that humans do not constitute a distinct family, nor even a distinct genus, but belong in the same genus as common and pigmy chimpanzees. Given that our genus name was proposed first, they have advanced the idea that there are three species of genus *Homo* on the planet today: the common chimpanzee, *Homo troglodytes;* the pigmy chimpanzee, *Homo paniscus;* and finally the human chimpanzee, *Homo sapiens.*[17]

Nor does the thesis of a difference in kind become more tenable if, rather than to that modern substitute for Aristotelian essence that is genetic code, one turns to empirically ascertainable psychological characteristics. Recently, a pluralistic approach incorporating human phenomenology, nonhuman behavior, functional-evolutionary arguments and physiology led many authors to assert that all mental phenomena we find in humans can be found in the other animals, and that the most important capacities traditionally conceptualized as all-or-nothing—self-consciousness, capacity for autonomy, rationality, capacity for moral agency and so on—are instead multidimensional and gradational.[18] All this well suits not only that idea of evolutionary continuity that philosophers so often set aside when it comes to defending the moral superiority of the members of our species but also another aspect of Darwinian theory. For if the randomness of genetic mutations yields divergence, natural selection can yield convergence. Within the same environment, evolution tends to "repeat" in broad outline the best survival strategies: think of the similarity between the basic forms of the dolphin (a mammal) and of the shark (a fish), due to their common need to move fast through the water, or of the appearance of wings in beings as different as insects, birds, and bats. Since the mental capacities in question are obviously traits endowed with great adaptive value,[19] one can reasonably suppose that, under suitable circumstances, they will be repeatedly selected.

In the light of this, it seems plausible to conclude that, within the contemporary scientific framework, there is no way of upholding the existence of a categorical difference between humans and non-humans. But if this is so, there is no capacity that has never belonged to animals and which humans could "retain when disabled." On the whole, both the specific appeal to the idea that some beings can have, or retain, capacities not apparent to empirical observation—with its obvious reference to the contrast between ontological and phenomenal aspects—and the more general reference to qualitative leaps make it evident that Cohen's argument cannot stand without the introduction of metaphysical assumptions. As a consequence, Cohen has not succeeded in the endeavor to grant marginal humans the same status awarded to paradigmatic members of our species.

Retreat: Comparable Status, Different Treatment

The second path that can be followed to defend the appeal to membership in the human species as a criterion for the attribution of a superior moral status lies in accepting in a preliminary way the argument from marginal cases, while seeking, however, to get around its implications. The result of this approach is a series of attempts to defend the view that, even in case nonparadigmatic humans and nonhuman animals at the same mental level should be prima facie granted comparable moral status, we would still be entitled to treat the two groups differently.

The Argument from Relations

What could entitle us to treat marginal human beings differently from nonhumans endowed with like psychological characteristics? Although we have just ruled out the answer "the fact that they are human" when the reference is to an alleged relevance of species membership, there is a different sense in which this very answer can be put forward. It is the sense suggested by Robert Nozick—an author who, despite being among the first to confront the question of our relations with nonhumans, ended up defending, as we already noticed, a form of speciesism. After criticizing "the inadequacy of a 'moral individualism' that looks only at a particular organism's characteristics" Nozick goes on stating that, in a satisfactory moral scheme,

> perhaps it will turn out that the bare species characteristic of simply being human . . . will command special respect only from other humans—this is an instance of the general principle that the members of any species may legitimately give their fellows more weight than they give members of other species (or at least more weight than a neutral view would grant them). Lions, too, if they were moral agents, could not then be criticized for putting other lions first.[20]

What is one to say about this argument? We are here confronted by an appeal to relational rather than intrinsic characteristics—an appeal that points, rather than at neutral reasons, at agent-dependent reasons. Basically, the underlying idea is that, in dealing with a set of moral patients who would in themselves deserve equal status, moral agents are entitled to grant preferential treatment to some because of the special relationships they have with them. We should always be suspicious of agent-dependent reasons, as they are more likely to conceal forms of bias than neutral reasons are. This is just the case with Nozick's thesis. To understand why, it suffices, along the lines of James Rachels's reply, to submit the argument to a simple test, consisting in adapting it to an intrahuman context.[21] Let us therefore reread Nozick in this light:

> perhaps it will turn out that the bare racial characteristic of simply being white . . . will command special respect only from other whites— this is an instance of the general principle that the members of any race may legitimately give their fellows more weight than they give members of other races (or at least more weight than a neutral view would grant them). Blacks, too . . . could not then be criticized for putting other blacks first.

Once referred to human beings, the "general principle" that Nozick defends loses any appeal it may have had, revealing its true nature as an implicit appeal to prejudice.

Something similar can be objected to another defense of differential treatment of humans and nonhumans at the same mental level that appeals to relational aspects. In its exemplary form, the argument is ascribable to Mary Midgley. After considering "the natural, emotional preference for one's own species over others which seems to underlie much conduct attacked as 'speciesist,' " Midgley—whose metaethical stance is naturalistic—goes on to claim to have "found reason to admit its existence and to treat it with considerable respect."[22] It is clear that, in this case as in the previous one, one could argue that also the preference for the members of one's own race is a natural, emotional preference.

Unlike what happens in the case of Nozick, however, this objection is not confined to the argument but points instead at a serious problem from which Midgley's approach as a whole suffers. We know that most analytic moral philosophers today accept the standard interpretation of Hume's Law, according to which it is not possible to infer matters of value from matters of fact. Some sorts of naturalistic theories, on the other hand, deny the existence of a gap between *is* and *ought,* and identify goodness or rightness with "natural" properties of things. In Midgley's case, in particular, what we are dealing with is a form of neo-Aristotelian naturalism, which makes reference to what it is to be a good human being and to perform good human acts. Midgley is convinced that such notions do not imply any metaphysical commitment and are explicable in purely natural terms. As a consequence, she argues that the facts from which conclusions about values can follow are biological facts concerning our nature, which can be determined by virtue of ethological research.

Now, the question in this context is, Whatever the general problems from which it may suffer, can this sort of naturalistic ethical approach ground a defense of human equality? One can doubt it. For what about the possible naturalness, for example, of rape or of male dominance? In the field of sociobiology, some authors do not hesitate to claim that these and other disquieting aspects of our social life are consequences of human nature. True, we cannot at present prove that the tendency to rape and male dominance is for our species a natural biological inclination. But if some day we reached the conclusion that it indeed is such, should we desist from morally blaming it? Should we stop endeavoring to minimize its effects? What would then become of the equal rights of women? On the whole, given the high risk of sanctioning various discriminatory attitudes it implies, it seems that Midgley's appeal to what "is natural" for the species can by no means be accepted by an advocate of humanism.

The Slippery Slope

If forms of scientifically updated Aristotelianism can hardly justify the view that, even in cases of comparable moral status, one can accord members of our species better treatment than that granted to members of other species, what about the different challenge coming from some versions of contractarian theory? A good example is the position of the very same Peter Carruthers we mentioned when considering the question of the neo-Cartesian revival. The version of contractarianism favored by Carruthers sees morality as the result of a hypothetical contract between rational agents, and it tries to justify a system of moral principles by showing that agents would agree on them in specified ideal circumstances.[23] One can clearly recognize here the Rawlsian schema, with the difference that Carruthers does not apply it merely to the problem of political justice but extends it to offer a general theory of morality.

While discussing the criteria for inclusion in the moral community, Peter Carruthers agrees that his specific contractarian requirement—the capacity for rational agency—would exclude nonrational humans. Nevertheless, he concludes that these humans, unlike nonhumans at the same mental level, should be accorded basic rights because "a rule that accorded rights in proportion to degree of rational agency *would* be wide open to creeping abuse" and could put at risk the rights of the contractors themselves.[24] In this case, the agent-dependent reason for differentiating the treatment of humans and nonhumans is no longer altruistic/empathetic, as was the case with Nozick and Midgley, but is instead self-interested, in agreement with the prevailing tendency within approaches based on contract.

The connection between Carruthers's thesis and the contractarian context in which it is inserted, however, does not go beyond this particular substantive aspect. From the formal point of view, the argument from the risk for right-holders is nothing but a specific version of the more general, and autonomous, slippery slope argument, according to which we should not take steps that, by their very nature, might lead to further steps at the end of which there is something we definitely want to avoid. Employed in the most various contexts, the slippery slope argument suffers from a serious structural weakness: it is based on an empirical assumption. The fact that certain steps might imply others has not the cogency of a logical derivation but must be experimentally proven each time it is used. Carruthers's argument too, therefore, is open to the classic challenge made to all arguments of this kind, which lies in questioning their actual applicability to the cases under discussion. And, as has often been emphasized, it is not always the case that when dealing with questions of moral status rational agents cannot draw sharp lines that can prevent the slope from becoming slippery.[25] Quite often, what happens is just the contrary: think of the clear distinction between rational agents that in slave societies made it possible to deny rights to slaves while maintaining them without any risks for their "masters." If this is so, Carruthers does not succeed in showing that the self-interest of rational agents should lead to a different treatment for humans and nonhumans at the same mental level.

Curiously, Rawls himself resorts, in order to admit all and only members of the species *Homo sapiens* to the sphere of equal justice, to an argument analogous to that of Carruthers. Confronting the subject of the basis of equality, he writes in fact:

> I assume that the capacity for a sense of justice is possessed by the overwhelming majority of mankind, and therefore this question does not raise a serious practical problem. That moral personality suffices to make one a subject of claims is the essential thing. We cannot go far wrong in supposing that the sufficient condition is always satisfied. Even if the capacity were necessary, it would be unwise in practice to withhold justice on this ground. The risk to just institutions would be too great.[26]

In other words, it is the risk that human beings actually endowed with moral personality may be unduly excluded from the sphere of justice that allegedly entitles us to include in that very sphere human beings lacking such requisite. But, apart from the fact that here too one might raise the objection that the danger for just institutions, far from being liable to be taken for granted, would have to be proven, the anomalous insertion of consequentialist considerations in an antiteleological theory such as Rawls's seems to confirm the feeling that the various forms of appeal to the risk for paradigmatic humans often are nothing but an ad hoc device for getting around the problem of marginal cases.[27]

The Appeal to Fairness

The attempts to differentiate the treatment of humans and nonhumans who are in theory accorded the same moral status so far presented seem rather evidently unsatisfactory. There is, however, within this same approach, an argument that appears to have some plausibility. It is the appeal to fairness. An especially clear formulation of it is offered by Stanley Benn in the context of a discussion of intrahuman egalitarianism: "We say it is unfair to exploit the deficiencies of the imbecile who falls short of the norm, just as it would be unfair, and not just ordinarily dishonest, to steal from a blind man."[28] The idea was taken up by Michael Wreen, who expressly employed it in the debate on speciesism to reject the demand for equal treatment for human marginal cases and nonhuman animals at the same mental level, and to confine fundamental rights to members of our own species.[29] Roughly speaking, we can express the argument as follows. Marginal humans are less endowed than normal humans through no fault of their own. Their situation, be it genetic or accidental, is (for the most part) fortuitous. It would be unfair for the moral claims of those human beings to be affected by such morally arbitrary factors. It would be unfair for the stronger, more intelligent members of our species to take profit of their vulnerability. Therefore, we should not treat them as we treat nonhuman animals.

To understand why the appeal to fairness is only apparently plausible, we should inspect it more closely. The core of the argument refers to the principle that it is wrong for the stronger to take profit of the fortuitous deficiencies of the weaker—and it is this idea that strikes a sympathetic chord in us. The principle is then applied to intrahuman relationships: we should not treat fortuitously impaired human beings differently from ourselves. So far so good. Then, however, a further element is added—nonhuman beings. The sphere of possible application of the principle is thus widened: other beings which are weaker than ourselves are introduced. But the appeal to fairness does not even consider a further extension of the principle. Nonhuman animals are directly introduced with a second-class moral status that plays the role of a negative element of comparison. It is easy to overlook this move, as it is obviously backed by current morality. But of course we should ask: Why shouldn't the principle apply to nonhumans too? In other words, why shouldn't we consider it unfair to take advantage of *their* vulnerability?

Given the structure of the argument, the answer can only be, Because their condition is not fortuitous. We are here close to Richards's already mentioned argument from fortuitousness, with the difference that while Richards lays stress on the general problem of treating individuals as individuals, apart from what the natural lottery has dealt them, what is emphasized in this context is the particular relational obligation not to take profit of others' weakness. Wreen's view, moreover, has the advantage of bringing to the fore the substantive character of the appeal to fairness that was somewhat blurred in Richards's argument.

In what sense, then, is being an impaired human individual fortuitous, while being a nonhuman individual is not? The argument seems to equivocate between two senses of "fortuitous." On the one hand, there is, so to speak, the statistical meaning, with respect to which the thesis has some plausibility: for if certain mental capacities are normal for our species, then doubtless to lack them is for a human at least more "fortuitous" than it is for a nonhuman belonging to a species for which these capacities are not the norm.[30] But if so interpreted, fortuitousness lacks ethical relevance, as is shown for example by the fact that we do not think we should treat a wounded civilian differently from a wounded soldier just because the former was less likely to be hit. On the other hand, there is the overtly moral sense of fortuitousness having to do with the contingency of a faultless vulnerability. Here, the idea that the appeal to fortuitousness holds only in the case of humans, far from being evident, requires a justification.[31] The argument from fairness, however, provides no independent reason for this judgment. Its conclusion is simply reached by taking for granted that the appeal to moral fortuitousness works in the case of intraspecies differences but not in the case of interspecies differences. But this is question-begging. An argument that was developed to offer a relational defense of the moral relevance of species membership cannot without circularity implicitly appeal to species membership in one of its premises. As a consequence of this, the conclusion obviously does not follow.

With the collapse of what promised to be the best founded among the attempts to avoid the implications of the argument from marginal cases, it seems plausible to conclude that the idea that membership in the human species may be the criterion for first-class moral status does not withstand critical examination. With this, the way is finally open to reconsider in an impartial way—that is, irrespective of any group membership, be it a matter of race, sex, or species—the problem of the possible internal structure of the moral community.

Chapter 5

■■

Welfare and the Value of Life

The criticisms of the humanist doctrine so far examined make up, as I have already noted, a line of argument that is shared, with variations, by all philosophical defenders of animal liberation. The idea that membership in the human species cannot be set up as a criterion for superior moral status is a common theoretical belief for authors with different backgrounds and different substantive propensities. Things change, however, when one turns to the constructive phase.

Redefining the moral community and the possible levels of status without inconsistency or prejudice is a difficult undertaking, but a theoretically fundamental one. In this chapter I will discuss the main proposals advanced by authors who have engaged in such an endeavor, coming from both of the normative positions that dominate contemporary moral philosophy—utilitarianism and the deontological family of rights-based theories.

A classification widely shared by those who accept the inclusive criterion of consciousness differentiates between two chief areas of interest for the definition of moral status: the sphere of obligations concerning welfare and the sphere of obligations concerning the continuation of life. According to most authors, the number of the beings that are owed duties concerning welfare is greater than the number of the beings that are owed duties concerning the protection of life. Initially, we shall retain such distinction. Accordingly, we shall first discuss possible comparative criteria regarding welfare and then examine the ones regarding the protection of life. A brief discussion of the concept of person closes the chapter. It may be useful on account of the particular role that this notion traditionally plays in the ethical categorization of beings.

Welfare

The notion of welfare, or well-being, is ambiguous. It is used sometimes in a narrow sense, in relation to momentary subjective states, and sometimes in a broad sense, with reference to a series of basic aspects ranging from freedom to physical integrity. Unless otherwise specified, I shall employ the concept in this latter sense. In other words, I shall include in it the main elements that can negatively and positively affect the course of a being's life, with the exception of the discontinuation of existence, that is, death. The welfare of an individual will thus consist in the satisfaction of a set of fundamental interests—the interest in not suffering, the interest in not being crippled or otherwise disabled, the interest in not being confined.

According to the principle of equality, like cases should be treated alike. This creates a presumption in favor of equal consideration of interests, and thus in favor of the maintenance of the one and only criterion of consciousness, and places the burden of proof on the shoulders of the defenders of hierarchical accounts. The problem to be addressed by those who want to establish different levels is then: what can cause the equally vital interests of different beings to be granted different consideration? If the interests are equally vital by definition, the difference must lie in the characteristics of the being. If it could be shown that either the presence of one or more favored characteristics—rationality, autonomy, self-consciousness—or, more generically, a greater mental complexity can justify a difference in the treatment of equal interests, one could then appeal to the possession of such attributes as the comparative criterion for a superior moral status.

*A Utilitarian Approach: The Criterion of
Consciousness and Aggregation*

An aggregative doctrine such as utilitarianism is naturally inclined to compare interests in a direct way, without emphasizing any further characteristics of the individuals whose interests they are. And, not surprisingly, this is the approach adopted by Peter Singer, to whom we owe the most convincing formulation of utilitarian theory in a nonspeciesist perspective. About the interest in not suffering, Singer writes:

> If a being suffers there can be no moral justification for refusing to take that suffering into consideration. *No matter what the nature of the being,* the principle of equality requires that its suffering be counted equally with *the like suffering*—insofar as rough comparisons can be made—of any other being. . . . To mark [the] boundary by some other characteristic like intelligence or rationality would be to mark it in an arbitrary manner.[1]

For Singer, in other words, what counts is what we might call the horizontal level: interests are to be directly compared with one another. The vertical level, that is, the kind of individual to whom the interests belong, does not come into play. Or, rather, it comes into play only in an indirect way, insofar as it affects the determination of the degree of similarity among the interests in question:

> If I give a horse a hard slap across its [*sic*] rump with my open hand, the horse may start, but it presumably feels little pain. Its skin is thick enough to protect it against a mere slap. If I slap a baby in the same way, however, the baby will cry and presumably feel pain, for its skin is more sensitive. So, it is worse to slap a baby than a horse, if both slaps are administered with equal force. But there must be some kind of blow—I don't know exactly what it would be, but perhaps a blow with a heavy stick—that would cause a horse as much pain as we cause a baby by slapping it with our hand. That is what I mean by "the same amount of pain.". . .[2]

The point is as important as it is often misunderstood. Various authors, Brian Barry among them[3], objected to Singer that whatever the relevant scales may be, the interests of members of different species will not come out as being of equal weight. What this objection fails to grasp is that Singer's principle of equal consideration states that equal weight should be given to equal interests. In other words, the equal weight of the involved interests is, so to speak, analytically true, and the only problem is the factual one of accurately assessing when the interests are in fact comparable.

In this sense, Singer's approach partially diverges from the most widespread classification of interests. Where the majority of authors distinguish between the main components of welfare—not suffering, physical integrity, and freedom—and all other interests, Singer sees a mass of specific interests to be singly evaluated and compared in turns. This implies that the degree of similarity can never be determined a priori but always requires an appeal to empirical data. One might think that, in this way, the difference between kinds of beings will turn up again like a bad penny, always leading, for instance, to the preeminence of beings endowed with greater mental complexity. This is not the case. As Barry's objection shows, it is relatively easy to bring into play prejudices and abstract evaluations when speaking of individuals, and even more so when speaking of groups of individuals. If, however, the weighting refers to interests, the situation changes. A classic example is offered once again by Singer when he compares the possible quantity of suffering a temporary imprisonment causes beings at different levels of mental complexity. If, he says, we are taking prisoners in wartime, we can explain to them that, while they must submit to capture, search, and confinement, they will not otherwise be harmed and will be set free at the conclusion of hostilities. If, however, we capture animals who have always lived free, we cannot explain that we are not threatening their lives—they cannot distinguish an attempt to confine them, for example, in order to treat them, from an attempt to kill, and the one causes them as much terror as the other.[4] In other words, the horizontal evaluation of single interests minimizes the influence of unjustified preconceptions and, by revealing that mental complexity can play very different roles with respect to the amount of frustration involved, does not leave the ground of equal consideration. The result is the ruling out of any difference in status and the confirmation of the single criterion for access to moral consideration—consciousness in the sense of possession of interests—as the only criterion for welfare as well.

What difference such an approach may mark is shown, among other things, by its implications for a practice that current morality virtually takes for granted. For it is on the basis of a simple, direct comparison between the interests involved—of great moment for the members of other species, confined, crippled, and killed, and of little consequence for human beings, who eat meat for a mere matter of taste—that Singer has condemned as ethically unacceptable the most rooted and widespread form of exploitation of nonhuman animals, that is, raising them for food.

There is, however, an aspect of utterly leaving individuals out of consideration that lends itself to an important criticism. According to utilitarianism, the aim of moral action is to bring about, or make likely, the best total balance of good over bad consequences—of pleasure over pain according to classical utilitarianism, of satisfaction over frustration of preferences according to the contemporary version for which Singer himself in the end opted. A fundamental objection to this all-inclusive calculation is that it doesn't sufficiently take into account the *separateness* of individuals. Such objection can be expressed in various contexts—Bernard Williams, for example, advances it with reference to moral agents, claiming that utilitarianism, by focusing on the overall consequences and not on those who achieve them, overlooks the aspect of personal integrity connected to individual moral action.[5] The aspect that concerns us here refers instead to moral patients. The idea is that an ethical doctrine that sees individuals as mere receptacles of that which is truly valuable—happiness, the satisfaction of preferences—however consistently egalitarian it might be at the level of access to consideration, will always be liable to be anti-egalitarian in its results. This means, in our case, that even if the interests of the cognitively less complex individuals enter into the calculation with the same weight as the like interests of the more complex beings, once the addition has been performed, it might be morally permissible to give the former differential treatment. If, for example, biomedical experimentation on severely intellectually disabled humans, taking all variables into account, side effects included, might lead to a greater balance of overall happiness over unhappiness, then it would turn out to be permissible.

At least two difficulties emerge here. The first concerns the possible institutionalized discrimination of nonparadigmatic groups. The second concerns instead the denial of the deeply intuitive idea that a fence should be erected around individuals that defends them from becoming mere instruments for the attainment of the common good. This latter aspect obviously affects any being, since the outcome of the felicific calculus can lead to sacrificing the interests of the intellectually most complex individuals as well. In the face of the charge of counterintuitivity raised against their theory, utilitarians have taken two lines. There are those—and Singer is one of them—who have counterattacked, arguing that intuitions are of no value in ethics because they can simply be the fruits of prejudices, of a bad upbringing, or of a lack of suitable information.[6] And there are those instead who have given a little ground, shifting from act utilitarianism, which assesses the consequences of individual actions, to rule utilitarianism, which takes into consideration the consequences, and therefore the felicific value, of rules of behavior.

Without going here into the details of a long and complex debate, it can be noticed that, evidently, rule utilitarianism narrows the gap with respect to theories of Kantian ascent, and to common sense as well. This is confirmed by the fact that, with Mill, this version of utilitarianism not only acknowledges the centrality of negative duties but is also able to incorporate those rights that Bentham described as mere nonsense.[7] Yet, various authors have underscored that rule utilitarianism, insofar as it does not give up seeing individuals as receptacles, has trouble accommodating the normative force of rights. The problem seems to be that utilitarian maximization, all things considered, cannot make room for the idea that rights entail what David Lyons acutely defined as an argumentative or justificatory threshold. If they wanted to do so, utilitarians would have to include an external factor, which does not follow either from the logic or from the implications of their perspective.[8]

A Deontological Approach: The Subject-of-a-Life Criterion and Side Constraints

Among the authors who criticized Peter Singer's positions from this standpoint, opposing utilitarianism with a nonspeciesist version of Kantianism, the American philosopher Tom Regan is probably the best known.[9] Regan is to be credited with the theoretical merit of attempting to recast in nonmetaphysical terms the Kantian idea of absolute worth—an attempt perhaps half-successful, and for this reason somewhat controversial. Regan expresses himself in the language of rights. He defines moral rights, along the lines of Joel Feinberg, as claims that are (a) validated by reference to sound moral principles, and (b) valid both as claims-to (a certain treatment) and as claims-against (some individuals).[10] Moral rights perform here the function of setting limits to utilitarian aggregation, preventing individuals from being sacrificed to promote general utility.

It is in this context that Regan introduces the notion of intrinsic value—or rather inherent value, as he prefers to call it since, in English-speaking philosophy, the attribute "intrinsic" is often referred to the value of mental states rather than individuals. There are, Regan claims, individuals who are endowed with inherent value, and such value should affect the way we treat them. Those who have inherent value are not simple receptacles of experiences and cannot be used as mere means to others' ends. The possession of inherent value originates the general right to a respectful treatment, that is, to a treatment that submits the overall calculation of consequences to side constraints. For Regan, therefore, the right to welfare, inclusive of freedom and bodily integrity, is subsumed under the right to respect.

Who has inherent/intrinsic value? To a like question, Kant had replied: rational natures (though he had then unjustifiedly shifted to human beings). Regan replies by offering the subject-of-a-life criterion. Individuals are subjects-of-a-life if they are endowed with a specific cluster of characteristics:

> beliefs and desires; perception, memory, and a sense of the future, including their own future; an emotional life together with feelings of pleasure and pain; preference- and welfare-interests; the ability to initiate action in pursuit of their desires and goals; psychophysical identity over time . . .[11]

It is the presence of this set of characteristics that underlies the attribution of inherent value to moral agents, Regan argues. He then goes on to observe that such presence can be identified in many human and nonhuman beings that are merely moral patients, and that this is a morally relevant similarity that leads to the rejection of the agent-patient parity principle.

Not surprisingly, Regan defines with Kantian terminology inherent value as a postulate. Although Kant didn't in fact include intrinsic value ("absolute worth") among the postulates of practical reason, the link between the two notions is evident: both perform the function of setting limits to the instrumental use of some beings. This parallel has, I believe, a strong heuristic value with respect to Kant. Already, Schopenhauer had observed that the notion of end-in-itself was problematic:

> But I must say frankly that *"to exist as an end in oneself"* is an unthinkable expression, a *contradictio in adjecto*. To be an end or aim means to be willed. Every aim or end in view exists only in reference

to a will, and is the end of the will, that is (as I have said), the direct motive of it. Only in this relation has the concept *end* any meaning, which it loses as soon as it is torn away. But this essential relation necessarily excludes all *in itself*.[12]

If, however, the notion of end-in-itself is conceived of as the extremity of a continuum at whose opposite end there is the complete lack of side constraints—be it a matter of being used for others' selfish purposes or of being included in the utilitarian aggregative calculus—its meaning becomes clearer. The significance of the role played by the anti-utilitarian argument appears to be confirmed by what Kant writes for instance in defense of the retributivist view of sanction:

> Judicial punishment can never be used merely as a means to promote some other good . . . The penal law is a categorical imperative; and woe to him who creeps through the serpent-windings of utilitarianism to discover some advantage that may discharge him from the justice of punishment. . . .[13]

In this perspective, Kantian intrinsic value appears in a new light: far from having an alleged objective foundation, it actually takes shape as the value that some individuals grant to themselves beyond, and in opposition to, any value they might have for others, and becomes therefore an attribute of subjectivity—the end-in-itself becomes *end-for-itself*. Such an interpretative thread emerges rather clearly from what Regan writes about the criterion for the attribution of inherent value:

> Now, those who satisfy this criterion are the subjects-of-a-life that is experientially better or worse *for them,* logically independently of their utility for others and their being the object of another's interests. Those who satisfy this condition, in short, are individuals *who have an experiential welfare*—whose experiential life fares well or ill, depending on what happens to, or is done to or for, them.[14]

Incidentally, it seems natural to ask in the face of this why Regan's notion of inherent value has been the object of charges of obscurity and clumsiness one would hardly find in the case of the Kantian notion of intrinsic value. And the most plausible answer seems to be that when the attribution of value goes beyond the boundaries of the human species theories must satisfy a higher standard of evidence than the one usually required in other cases.

What is, then, the outcome of attributing the right to a respectful treatment to subjects-of-a-life as far as the moral classification of individuals' welfare is concerned? Essentially, it is the creation of a two-level moral community, in which the interest in welfare (in freedom, in physical integrity) of some beings counts for more than the interest in welfare of some others, in the sense that it cannot be sacrificed in cases in which it is permissible to sacrifice the latter. Since, moreover, Regan conceives of inherent value as a categorical value that doesn't allow of degrees,[15] the inner circle of the moral community—the one reserved for subjects-of-a-life—not only designates a superior moral status but also has, within its boundaries, an egalitarian structure. In other words, as regards welfare interests, vertical evaluation—that is, the evaluation that refers to the kind of individuals to whom the interests belong—comes into play to define the area where the right to respect applies. Once it has established this distinction, it disappears, leaving in its place horizontal evaluations that directly compare interests with one another, with side constraints in the case of subjects-of-a-life, and in a tendentially aggregative way when it comes to all other beings.[16] Basically, what Regan propounds is the traditional two-level system, with the difference, however, that first-class moral status is not restricted to moral agents (and, by an unjustified extension, to all and only human beings) but is also granted to individuals who are only moral patients—more precisely, to all normal nonhuman mammals aged one or more, and to a large number of human marginal cases, whom a consistent application of the agent-patient parity principle would have excluded.

As should be clear from this very brief analysis, in rights theories full moral status is characterized by the presence of constraints on maximizing aggregation. Such constraints affect the normative framework and, in particular, the understanding of the conflict of interests. For an utterly aggregative position, every situation involves a conflict of interests: the duty to choose the maximizing action implies not only the permissibility but also the obligatoriness of interference with respect to all the beings involved—from which the fundamental equivalence, for utilitarians, of acts and omissions. The result of this is that the whole of moral life is, so to speak, a lifeboat, where one must perpetually decide who is to be saved and who is to be sacrificed. In a rights-based moral approach, on the contrary—at least in the case of strong moral rights of Kantian descent—the basic interests of m ral patients are protected from almost any form of aggregation, and conflict is therefore circumscribed to emergency situations in which all the beings involved are exposed to an equal and unavoidable danger.[17] Regan's approach involves the novelty of extending this more restricted understanding of conflict, usually confined to the intrahuman sphere, to the relationships with members of other species.

A concrete example can clarify what this means. Biomedical research that makes use of animals is normally presented as a lifeboat situation. It is claimed, that is, that animal experimentation is the unavoidable result of a choice between the welfare of some individuals (usually human) and the welfare of other individuals (invariably nonhuman). Human experimentation, on the other hand, is seen in a different light. In this case, we do not deem it permissible to pick out some individuals in order to use them as experimental subjects in laboratory researches by which other individuals may benefit. When it comes to humans, far from appealing to unavoidable choices between beings, we debar as immoral what we consider as an unacceptable form of instrumentalization. What lies at the root of such a difference in approach? Once again, Nozick's reading of current morality as an undeclared mixture of Kantianism for humans and utilitarianism for animals can be enlightening here. While in the case of humans, where Kantianism applies, basic moral rights act, as Ronald Dworkin put it, as trump cards able to prevent any purely aggregative move,[18] when it comes to the second-class ethical condition to which nonhuman animals are relegated, where utilitarianism applies, the practice of routinely sacrificing the welfare of some beings for the benefit of others is portrayed as an unavoidable conflict of interests. This normative stratification, however, is in no way defended: rather, the double standard is surreptitiously introduced, and the inconsistency goes unobserved only because it is implicitly taken for granted that nonhumans, unlike humans, already fall within the number of mere resources.

Of course, a consistently utilitarian approach like Singer's, which excludes any arbitrary distinction between individuals on the basis of their species membership, does away with the theoretical/practical dichotomy between human experimentation and animal experimentation. It does away with it, however, in the sense of putting the conflict of interests at the center of the debate on biomedical research on human subjects as well, by ventilating the possibility of introducing the maximizing calculus also with respect to members of our species. Just the opposite happens with deontological approaches such as Regan's. The introduction of an equal strong moral right to welfare entails in fact a significant shrinking of what is usually seen as the area of conflict in the case of nonhumans. As a consequence of this, comparably to what happens in the human instance, the institutionalized reduction of some beings to mere laboratory tools does not appear as the unavoidable outcome of a choice among individuals but rather as an unacceptable infringement of moral rights. This has, among other things, the result of overturning the traditional approach to the problem of animal experimentation, raising in relation to this practice the same ethical objections that are put forward against human experimentation.

What is one to say, on the other hand, about Regan's more general reconstruction of the moral community? Apparently, the subject-of-a-life comparative criterion does not comply with the prerequisite of contextual relevance. As we have seen, Regan describes the subjects-of-a-life as those beings that have beliefs and desires, memory, a sense of the future, an emotional life, preference-interests and welfare-interests, and the ability to pursue their goals.[19] What, then, about a being that lacks a sense of future but is endowed, for example, with welfare interests? Why should its welfare interests be treated differently from the analogous interests of subjects-of-a-life? What has the sense of future to do with the interest in not suffering? Regan is clearly aware of this problem and lets his perplexities come to light in two ways. On the one hand, he states that the selected criterion is sufficient but not necessary.[20] On the other, as it also happens with the brief passage quoted above, when defending the individual from utilitarian aggregation, he often mentions as the morally relevant characteristic not the whole cluster of capacities which defines the subject-of-a-life but rather the mere possession of that *experiential welfare* that points at the criterion of consciousness. Such cautions and hesitations are evidence of an unsolved difficulty as for the relationships between mental complexity and specific interests.

A Mixed Theory: Divergence of the Criteria and Prima Facie Duties

This problem is fully brought to light by the last approach to welfare we shall take into consideration. Formulated by David DeGrazia, this approach does not completely fall within the sphere of either deontological or consequentialist theories. What DeGrazia has developed is a sort of mixed account that, along the lines of David Ross's intuitionism, revolves around the notion of prima facie duties, that is, of duties that carry some moral weight but must be mutually balanced and must take into account possible ethically relevant variables.[21] To such a doctrine, obviously pluralistic, DeGrazia then imparts a Rawlsian tone through the recourse to a coherentist method. In short, coherentism opposes foundationalism. Rather than construing ethical systems as chains of justifications that at a certain point terminate in one or more ultimate (exactly, foundational) beliefs, coherentism sees them as complex sets of beliefs that can only justify each other in a mutual way.[22] The leading form of coherentism is precisely the method of reflective equilibrium presented in John Rawls's *A Theory of Justice,* on the basis of which one begins with a set of considered beliefs, then formulates general principles that may account for them, and finally revises both principles and beliefs in the light of each other until an equilibrium is attained.

It is apparent that such a method carries a specific risk that is especially serious when dealing with moral reform—the risk of incorporating, through the beliefs one accepts as a somehow intuitive starting-point, partialities or group biases. Aware of this problem, DeGrazia defends a type of coherentism in which the task of functioning as an antidote for possible prejudices is assigned on the one hand to the appeal to universalizability, and on the other to a constant empirical verification based on close comparison with nonmoral background theories such as psychology, the social sciences, and evolutionary biology. Such theoretical commitments are consistently met through the philosophical discussion of recent achievements within the domain of cognitive disciplines, as well as the review of the leading contemporary accounts of prudential value, that is, of what makes the experiential life of a conscious being go better or go worse.

As regards welfare, which is clearly subdivided into the three basic components of nonsuffering, bodily integrity, and freedom, DeGrazia defends in the first instance—starting essentially from the principle of universalizability—a presumption in favor of equal consideration, which is defined as the attribution of equal moral weight or significance to relevantly similar interests, irrespective of the cognitive complexity of the interest-bearers.[23] Nonetheless, he believes that such a presumption can be reversed. How?

As we have seen in the case of Regan's theory, the traditional path of *immediately* referring to the presence of one or more favored characteristics—autonomy, rationality, moral agency, or some other—appears unsatisfactory. The prerequisite of contextual relevance prevents any appeal to comparative criteria that are not directly relevant for each basic aspect of welfare, and it seems implausible to maintain that, for example, a nonrational or nonautonomous human being, if tortured or crippled, comes to a lesser harm than a normal adult human being does. In the light of all this, DeGrazia opts for a different approach.

Basically, what he advances is a *mediate* appeal to characteristics. The core idea is that all aspects of welfare, in addition to being valuable in themselves, can also have an instrumental value.[24] Individuals whose welfare is impaired, DeGrazia argues, are not only directly harmed but are also deprived, to a greater or lesser degree, of the ability, and of the strength, to pursue their goals—in other words, they suffer indirect losses. These losses have a prudential value that varies according to the different characteristics of the individuals. So the presumption in favor of equal consideration for welfare interests can be undermined and might give way to the gradualist principle that the greater a being's cognitive complexity, the more moral weight its interests should receive.[25] Since, however, the occurrence of such a possibility cannot be generically assumed but has to be ascertained case by case, DeGrazia examines separately each of the three elements into which he has subdivided welfare.

The most unequivocal appraisal concerns the causing of suffering. In relation to this aspect, DeGrazia asserts, the same standards are to be applied whatever the nature of the being whose interests are in question. The conclusion reached about bodily integrity is not very different: in the terms proper to a pluralistic theory, it results in a virtually absolute presumption against disabling, or in any other way rendering incapable of functioning in a normal way, all sentient beings, irrespective of their nature. This means that in both cases the criterion remains the inclusive one of consciousness. And the reason for this, DeGrazia argues, lies in the fact that when it comes to suffering and mutilation the value-in-itself of the goods involved is such as to virtually drive any possible instrumental value off the stage.

It is with the transition to the component revolving around the pair of opposites freedom/confinement that the argument takes a different turn. After defining confinement as the imposition of external constraints on movement that significantly interfere with one's ability to live a good life, DeGrazia suggests in fact that in the case of deprivation of freedom, instrumental value cannot be entirely overlooked. Concretely, this means that the freedom interests of the cognitively simpler beings may be granted a less-than-equal moral weight, on the basis of the idea that—owing to their allegedly lesser capacity for satisfaction—the prudential disvalue their confinement causes them is lower than that caused to cognitively more complex beings.[26]

Clearly, a position that does not attribute moral relevance to the species boundary must in this connection confront the problem of human marginal cases. In other words, it must in general be prepared to accept the hypothesis that one or more of the welfare interests of, for example, a child with Down's syndrome, can be discounted when measured against the like interests of a normal adult. This conclusion is difficult to accept for those who, like DeGrazia, attribute philosophical weight to intuitions. True, in a mixed theory side effects can play a role, and DeGrazia does not fail to appeal to two among them: the possible misery caused to other beings emotionally bound to the individuals in question, and what he defines as the "effects on the fabric of the moral community," that is, the risks for the system of prohibitions in force among beings endowed with paradigmatic moral status.[27] And yet, he himself raises doubts about this solution:

> One might argue that the consequences of giving [human marginal cases] less-than-equal consideration are so pernicious as to justify giving them, in practice, equal consideration. . . . As noted in our critique of contractarianism, that move has problems involving the implication that their status depends on contingencies in a way that other humans' status does not, and involving the possibility that we are wrong about the existence of such contingencies.[28]

It is largely, although not only, because of this general unwillingness to give up the egalitarian presumption in the case of marginal humans that DeGrazia opts for setting aside the instrumental value of welfare with respect to suffering and mutilation. And it is perhaps because of a similar but reverse motive that he defends instead the possibility of multiple standards with respect to freedom interests. The idea, in short, is that, in the case of intellectually disabled human beings, there are justified forms of paternalistic coercion—measures, in other words, that restrict freedom in the interest of the subject. Yet, if one claims that "to the extent that we can separate out freedom interests in practice, for a large class of sentient animals . . . the presumption against confining them is ordinarily weaker"[29] than the presumption against confining cognitively more complex beings—if one defends, that is, a divergence in the criteria when it comes to the interest in not being confined—the way is obviously open to a *nonpaternalistic* deprivation of liberty, and therefore to a less-than-equal consideration, in the case of marginal humans as well.

In one respect, DeGrazia's tendency to create within welfare a divergence between equal consideration, and hence maintenance of the criterion of consciousness, and multiplicity of standards, and hence introduction of a gradualist comparative criterion linked to mental complexity, can be read in a structural way—as the product, that is, of the encounter between the utilitarian, horizontal and egalitarian, approach, and the Kantian, vertical and hierarchical, approach. In another respect, however, it points to problems that appear most decisively with the question of the interest in life. It will be in such context, therefore, that we shall go back to the question of the possible introduction of comparative criteria for welfare and, in particular, for freedom.

When Killing Is Wrong

It has been observed that, whatever the differences among theoretical approaches and among the results reached with respect to welfare, most authors end by agreeing on at least two views. The first is that the harm that death is is not equal for all moral patients but varies according to the presence or absence of one or more psychological characteristics. The second is that the crucial characteristics must be somehow connected with the capacity for self-consciousness.

As we shall see, the situation is more complex. Nonetheless, this suggestion can be a good starting point to unravel the complexities of a question that animal liberation theorists share with bioethicists, and which is often expressed in terms of the problem of the right to life.

The Immediate Appeal to Self-consciousness

In what sense can self-consciousness be relevant to the wrongness of taking life? A first answer is offered by preference utilitarianism. As we know, according to this recent version of the utilitarian doctrine, the nonmoral good to be maximized by our actions does not lie in the narrow Benthamite notion of pleasure but lies instead, more generally, in the satisfaction of individual preferences. The consequences on the basis of which an action can be deemed right or wrong, therefore, no longer revolve around the pleasure/pain pair but instead around the satisfaction/frustration of preferences pair.

On this view, which, as we have seen, was adopted by Peter Singer among others, only if a being has a preference for its continued existence is the fact of killing it (painlessly) the infliction of a harm,[30] that is, the frustration of a preference. But in order to have the desire to go on living, a being must be aware of itself as a distinct entity, endowed with a past and a future, that is, it must consider itself as existing in time. Self-consciousness plays here a direct role, immediately linked to the possibility of conceiving of one's death as the discontinuance of one's existence, and of dreading such discontinuance. From this perspective, a being that is unable to consider itself as existing in time can neither understand nor fear the possibility of being deprived of its future existence, and hence does not experience a frustration if it is killed. Hence, the comparative criterion of self-consciousness.

This criterion, often presented as all-or-nothing, is in fact central to reflection on the morality of taking life even in normative theories other than utilitarianism, and many of the authors who have discussed the morality of abortion and euthanasia make reference to it. For example, the American philosopher Donald VanDeVeer writes in the context of a discussion of the morality of euthanasia for seriously defective human infants: "In the absence of a more persuasive view, I believe we must conclude that . . . beings lacking a capacity for self-awareness lack a right to life."[31]

What is one to say about the direct appeal to self-consciousness as a comparative criterion for access to the protection of life? The first thing to note is that it seems to be able to meet the prerequisite of contextual relevance. For if one keeps to the idea that an interest is morally relevant only when it is directly related to the corresponding desire or preference, it is reasonable to maintain that the possession, or lack, of the desire to go on living, or of the preference for a continued existence, and consequently the possession of the prerequisite of self-consciousness, make the difference with respect to the harm that death is. It is, however, in this very premise that the problem from which this approach suffers is hidden. What about the idea that, since we don't have the conscious desire to breathe oxygen, we would not be harmed were we deprived of oxygen? Perhaps, such a notion of harm is too narrow.

The Mediate Appeal to Characteristics

James Rachels writes:

> When we say that something is valuable "to someone," we might mean three things. First, we might mean that someone *believes* the thing is valuable; or secondly, we might mean that someone consciously *cares* about it. . . . But there is a third, more straightforward understanding of what is meant . . . In saying that something is valuable for someone, we might simply mean that *this person would be worse off without it*. It is important to notice that this third sense is independent of the first two. The loss of something might in fact be harmful to someone even though they were ignorant of this fact and consequently did not care about it.[32]

The distinction drawn here echoes the one made by other authors—particularly Steve Sapontzis—between the possibility of valuing something or taking an interest in something on the one hand, and the fact of having an interest in something on the other.[33] It appears as well in slightly different forms in varied contexts—think for example of the contrast, within the more general debate on rights, between "choice theory," which connects the possession of a right to the power to assert it or to waive it knowingly, and "interest theory," which grounds the right simply in the benefit one derives from it.[34]

Such analysis directs us toward an alternative interpretation of the harm of killing. According to this interpretation, the value of life is *instrumental:* the continuation of one's existence is important not because it is preferred or valued in itself but because it enables one to have all that is valuable to a subject—experiences, emotions, activities, relationships, projects. We have already met the notion of "biographical life" in another context. Here, it helps to shed light on a hypothesis other than the one suggested by those who focus on the possible *direct* harms caused by death: the idea that the prohibition against killing should be related to the *indirect* harm represented by the loss of all prudential value an existence may contain.

The plausibility of this idea seems to undermine the line of thought that denies that non-self-conscious beings can be harmed by death. Is there a way to correct the approach based on self-consciousness so as not to deny the existence of indirect harm? Giving prominence to subtler forms of relationship with the self, Michael Tooley argued that what grounds the right to life is the property of being the subject of nonmomentary interests, and that this property implies the possession of the concept of a continuing self or mental substance. On this basis, he defended the permissibility of abortion, and, within limits, of infanticide.[35] It is clear that, formulated in this way, Tooley's argument doesn't embody the view that an interest is morally relevant only when it is directly related to the corresponding desire, thus avoiding an unjustifiably restricted notion of harm. And yet, the attempt to reconcile the idea of indirect harm with the idea of a relationship with the self appears to yield a conception of the crucial property—namely, that of being a subject of nonmomentary interests—that is exceedingly demanding. As it has been noted, it is implausible to make such property depend on factors not only cognitively exacting but also as culturally relative as the possession, and self-attribution, of the concept of a continuing self.[36] This seems to suggest the abandonment of any reference to the relationship with the self in favor of the argument defended by Rachels.

If one does this, the terms of the problem as they have been stated by DeGrazia will clearly reappear. And, in fact, DeGrazia himself presents the paradigmatic form of the argument for the attribution of instrumental value to life in combination with the like argument concerning welfare, albeit with the difference that, in the case of life—seen as a prerequisite for anything that is ultimately valuable for individuals—instrumental value tends to hold the center of the stage, leaving little or no space for value-in-itself. The same basic idea can be found more or less explicitly in many authors belonging both to the deontological and to the consequentialist school. It is evident that such a view rules out an immediate role for self-consciousness, which is no longer the privileged criterion for inclusion among the beings for which death can be a harm. What comes to the fore is, rather, the idea of a subjectivity capable of complex experiences, to which self-consciousness belongs as a component among others. For the approaches that attribute an instrumental value to life, in other words—though with some exceptions—the criterion tends to be the gradualist one of mental complexity. Starting from this common element, positions differentiate, ranging on the basis of their specific approach to prudential value from strongly perfectionist accounts to a widespread prohibition against killing. It is to these approaches that we will now turn.

The Value of Life: Qualitative Theories

At the basis of the view that the harm that death is is connected with the instrumental value of life lies, as we have noted, prudential value, that is, the value, from the subject's point of view, of all the opportunities for satisfaction that the fact of being alive provides. The problem is thus: how can this particular value be weighed? How can comparisons be made?

A traditional solution is represented by some sort of appeal to qualitative differences. John Stuart Mill's position comes immediately to mind. As it will be remembered, Mill, claiming that it is "better to be a human being dissatisfied than a pig satisfied, better to be Socrates dissatisfied than a fool satisfied," introduces the idea that there are elements within prudential value—in his case pleasures, but they might also be relationships, activities, and the like—that are qualitatively superior to others, and he assigns the task of identifying them to the judgment of "all or almost all who have experience" of the entire range. We know, however, that this solution runs into the problem of the dissenting judges: how can the appeal to the majority—or even to the near totality—be sufficient to justify overriding the individual's judgment? Obviously, the same also holds if one applies the theory of qualitative differences to the question of the comparison between lives: within a subjective approach, no intersubjective agreement can prevail over a possible dissenting viewpoint. If, having tried both the life of the fool and the life of the philosopher, I find the first to be preferable, no one has the authority to claim that I am wrong.

But if it is true that the difficulties from which Mill's proposal suffers stem from the fact that it stands within the domain of subjective accounts, it seems that the only way to go on defending the thesis of qualitative differences lies in leaving the subjective viewpoint in order to venture on the path of objectivity. Something that points in this direction can be found in the work of the American utilitarian philosopher Raymond Frey, in the past an advocate of selective experimentation on nonhumans and now led by his acceptance of a nonspeciesist approach to consider also the possibility of forms of invasive experimentation on human beings.

The argument Frey puts forward is actually rather complex and seems to lend itself both to a subjective and to an objective interpretation. Obviously, as we are dealing with an author of a utilitarian bent, a reading of his view in the terms of a subjective approach would seem more pertinent. Congruent with this reading would be the hedonistic assertion that "the value of a life is a function of its quality, its quality a function of its richness, and its richness a function of its scope or potentiality for enrichment."[37] Nonetheless, there are forms of utilitarianism, such as Moore's ideal version, according to which some things—beauty, pleasure, friendship, knowledge—are objectively good, or good in themselves. Frey seems to be arguing along these lines when, for example, he observes that autonomy as control "is crucial to a further and significant dimension of value to our lives."[38] This and other similar passages give one the feeling that Frey not only drops the criterion of mental complexity in favor of the appeal to a single characteristic but also attributes to the characteristic in question *a special weight,* to the effect that the life of a being endowed with it objectively has greater value than the life of a being lacking it.

In a sense, such a position is interesting just because of its ambiguities. Although for quite some time English-speaking moral philosophy did not show great interest in objective theories of value, the situation is now changing, with the result that objectivism often reappears not in the open manner that has distinguished continental ethics—think of the traditional attribution of intrinsic value to rationality—but in a more disguised way. What, then, about the idea that a specific characteristic—in this case, the capacity for autonomy, but it might also be just rationality, or something else—can confer a further dimension of value on life?

A problem that immediately arises is that Frey's view is marked by a serious ambiguity. Referring to "autonomy as control," Frey actually seems to maintain that some lives are endowed with greater value as a result of the fact that they are led autonomously. When discussing the value of life, however, it is important to draw a distinction between two questions that are often mixed up. One thing is the (possible) objective intraindividual hierarchy among the potential lives of the same kind of beings; quite another is the (possible) interindividual objective hierarchy among the lives of different kinds of beings. The former refers to *accidental* factors, in that it concerns life choices, or life opportunities; the latter refers to *structural* factors, in that it concerns the capacities of individuals. As Steve Sapontzis has aptly observed, not to understand this point—to mistake, that is, a comparison *between different actualizations of the same capacities* with a comparison *between differing capacities*—amounts to making a category mistake.[39]

It is clear that the former comparison does not allow one to establish a hierarchy among different kinds of beings, since nobody can live the life of a different kind of being. If I am structurally devoid of the capacity to be autonomous, it makes no sense to judge me on the grounds of the absence from my life of the actualization of this capacity. Frey must therefore opt for the latter comparison—that is, for an account based on the structural presence (or on the level of structural presence) of the favored capacity. And yet, this option too suffers from a serious difficulty.

Such difficulty lies in the crucial fact that the adoption of the objective viewpoint implies that the alleged qualitative variations in the value of lives have no longer to do with prudential value. This claim may seem odd, since there exists a tradition of objective interpretation of prudential value that goes at least as far back as Aristotle. Yet, such tradition was made possible only by the recourse to the notion of eudaemonia—that is to say, by the appeal to the idea that happiness (prudential value) and virtue (nonprudential value) coincide. It is obvious that, in this perspective, to say that the life of a being, if characterized by the presence of morally favored capacities—or, for that matter, by a greater actualization of these capacities—is more valuable, means also to say that it is a happier life, or an experientially better life. But if one gives up the specific eudaemonistic viewpoint, the objective interpretation of the value of lives loses all connection with the individual's experiential state.

If, then, an objective approach such as the one that might be attributed to Frey implies a parting from prudential value, how are the judgments on the alleged qualitative variations among the lives of different kinds of beings determined? The answer can only be: on the basis of the idea that the existence of characteristics and of beings of such kind is somehow good for the universe. In other words, the fact that there are autonomous beings must be seen, in an absolute sense, as preferable to the fact that there are no such beings. This cannot but point at some specific worldview. But of course this takes us back to the problem we have already tackled while criticizing the idea of intrinsic value. When it comes to questions as fundamental and general as those concerning moral status, it is arbitrary to draw general values from particular interpretations of reality. Why should an individual accept that her life is granted a lesser value then the lives of other individuals on the grounds of particular views about what is good for the universe? As DeGrazia aptly observes, in the face of such moves one cannot fail to recall "how often unverifiable metaphysical theses have been made in the name of treating some as naturally less deserving than others."[40] As a consequence of this, just like the subjective version, the objective version of the qualitative approach to the instrumental value of life does not withstand criticism.

A Detour on the Quality of Life

In passing, it is worth noting that the very distinction between *accidental* factors and *structural* factors that has proven to be relevant to the criticism of objective theories allows us to shed light on a perspective that is now quite widespread in bioethics. This is the so-called quality-of-life approach. Insofar as it opposes the traditional sanctity-of-life doctrine, the quality-of-life approach lays stress, rather than on the preservation of biological existence in itself, on the appraisal of the prudential value of the individual's life. Given that obviously such prudential value is not construed objectively, that is, in eudaemonistic terms, but rather subjectively, that is, in terms of satisfaction of interests, *accidental* factors refer in this context only to the levels of experiential value, excluding any reference to the possible presence or actualization of favored characteristics. In this perspective, advocates of the quality-of-life approach coherently defend the permissibility of voluntary euthanasia for fully competent individuals, as well as of nonvoluntary euthanasia for individuals who cannot understand the choice between life and death when life is unbearable from the very viewpoint of the beings involved—adults suffering from extremely serious diseases or newborn babies with fatal and painful deformities.

The doctrine in question is, however, more ambiguous than it may seem. From this initial reading, in fact, the authors involved often imperceptibly shift to a different account, where the focus is no longer on the levels of satisfaction (or frustration) as perceived by the individuals, but on the structural capacities of the individuals themselves. For example, Peter Singer writes in *Rethinking Life and Death* that the quality-of-life ethic demands that individuals are treated in accordance with their ethically relevant characteristics, and he mentions among these consciousness, the capacity for physical, social and mental interaction with other beings, having conscious preferences for continued life, and having enjoyable experiences.[41]

These characteristics are not homogeneous. There is in fact a categorical gap between the first three, which are structural, and the fourth, which is accidental. Of the first three, furthermore, the first one—consciousness—is the prerequisite for access to moral consideration, while the remaining two may mark different levels within such consideration. In particular, the capacity for interaction with others seems to stand for a whole set of possible perfectionist reference points, such as the intellectual or emotional level, and the possession of conscious preferences for the continuation of life is clearly linked to the problem of killing.

Evidently, it is possible to argue for the significance of all four factors, but, while doing this, one should make it clear that this interpretation of the idea of quality of life does not stop at actual prudential value—what is now my level of satisfaction or frustration—but extends to cover a presumed prudential value—what my level of satisfaction or frustration may allegedly be on the basis of the kind of being that I am. Now, if a judgment on the possible superiority of one of the ways in which individual lives can go can clearly be delivered from the subject's viewpoint, we saw in discussing Mill that a judgment about the possible superiority of the life of a being endowed with certain capacities compared to the life of a being lacking such capacities appears to require moving away from the level of subjectivity. Though often obscured by the fact that the most frequently cited case is that of the "human vegetable," in which the lack of a structural capacity like consciousness implies the absence of any possibility of experiences that are accidentally better or worse, the distinction between the two types of judgment remains.

Why is it important to underline this distinction, drawing a sharp line between the judgment on the accidental aspects and the judgment on the structural aspects of the lives of individuals? Because, if one doesn't do so, part of the self-evidence of the former judgment—that a happy life is superior to an unhappy one—is surreptitiously conveyed to the latter—that the life of a more complex being is superior to the life of a less complex being—and, consequently, it is possible to get around the justificatory difficulties the latter judgment involves.

The Value of Life: Quantitative Theories

Indeed, Singer himself, albeit in a different context, advances a proposal of justification. After asserting that even conscious life may, on the basis of his version of utilitarianism, have some value, though inferior to that of self-conscious life, he sets himself the problem of identifying a viewpoint starting from which it might be possible to outline a hierarchical order of the lives of different kinds of beings within a subjective outlook.

In doing this, he parts with Mill in two respects. The first, and fundamental, point concerns the approach to prudential value. Singer in fact replaces the appeal to qualitative differences with the idea that the instrumental value of individual lives is to be seen as a function of the quantity of prudential value (in terms of satisfaction of interests) that they may contain given the capacities of the beings that live them. This purely quantitative approach is an important step forward from Mill's approach, in that it does away with the problems attendant on the comparison of qualitatively different elements.

The second respect concerns Mill's appeal to the competent judge. While discussing this solution, Singer declares himself unsatisfied with it and opts instead for the idea of hypothetical choice. In short, his method can be described as follows: first, one should picture one's life, imagining it as "about as good as [a human life] can reasonably be expected to be on this planet"; then one should try to identify oneself with the being with which one wants to make the comparison, imaginatively attributing to it an equally good life; finally, one should seek to enter a third state in which one remembers both one's own existence and that of the other being and should then draw the comparison. The existence that one would choose in such a position is the one endowed with greater value, and, according to Singer, "the more highly developed the conscious life of the being, the greater the degree of self-awareness and rationality," the more one would prefer that kind of life.[42] Within this framework, the subjective viewpoint of the beings in question is not entirely eliminated, since it is taken as a starting point; however, it soon gives way to the, so to speak, subjective superindividual viewpoint that is introduced by hypothesizing a third, equidistant and neutral being.

Is this method more satisfactory than Mill's? One may doubt it. First of all, the idea that one can fully grasp the inner horizon of another being—Singer mentions once more a horse—is, at the least, empirically implausible. What does a human (the plain, though unspoken, hero of Singer's conjectural adventure) know of typically equine pleasures? How can we imagine what it is like to be a horse "frolicking with other horses, drinking from a pond on a hot day, eating sugar cane, and the like?"[43] Second, it is difficult to conceive of a truly neutral superindividual viewpoint: in order to make choices, one needs to be already endowed with preferences. In the case involved, either the preferences are neither human nor equine—and then it is hard to understand where they come from; or they are de facto human because the being engaging in the hypothetical choice is human—and it is dubious that this can help implying forms of partiality. Singer concludes:

> We cannot defend [the claim that the life of every being has equal value] by saying that every being's life is all-important *for it,* since we have now accepted a comparison which takes a more objective . . . stance.[44]

But this is question-begging. What is in question is just whether it is possible and/or reasonable to make this comparison, and therefore the comparison itself cannot be introduced into the argument without circularity.

These problems, however, concern solely the device of hypothetical choice. They do not affect those elements—subjective account, quantitative approach—that lie at the basis of the view. Can we maintain these elements within a different framework? In other words, is there still a possibility to defend, as regards the superior moral status connected with the protection of life, that gradualist comparative criterion linked to mental complexity that the qualitative approach has proven to be unable to justify? It is important to ascertain this point, not least because it seems undeniable that many authors dealing with the morality of abortion, euthanasia, or embryo experimentation proceed in this direction, arguing for a subjective/quantitative account that defines a hierarchy of lives not only starting from their actual, present prudential value, but also on the basis of the scope and intensity of the experiential content their structural characteristics make possible.

It is evident that, as was the case with welfare, the consequences of a hierarchical classification of the value of the lives of different kinds of beings will vary according to the specific substantive framework. For utilitarianism, granting lives a graduated value means affording in general different protection to different existences. In other words, less valuable lives can be preferentially taken on the grounds of an appeal to the (greater) benefit of other beings. Though the exact type of minimum protection offered will vary according to the favored version—lesser in the case of act utilitarianism, and greater in the case of rule utilitarianism that, as we have already noted, is less distant from deontological theories—such a possibility cannot, for theoretical reasons, be excluded; and, within a perspective that has given up bias in favor of our species, it might sometimes even lead to the killing of marginal human beings, for example, for organ harvesting.[45] For rights-based theories, on the other hand—given that the individual existences of beings that have basic rights can never be used as mere means to others' ends—once a being is granted a right to life, however weak, the problem of its preferential killing arises only within a more limited scope, that is, in special situations in which one must unavoidably decide which one is to be sacrificed among beings facing the same, impending danger.

Beyond the differences in their implications, however, the two main normative approaches show a remarkable convergence when it comes to justifying the idea that the lives of different kinds of beings can be classified on the basis of the amount of their possible prudential content. In the consequentialist field, for example, James Rachels, after arguing that death is a harm insofar as it deprives a being of its biographic life and that there is no reason the wrongness of taking life has to be an all-or-nothing matter, defends the idea that killing a being that has a more complex life is more objectionable than killing a being that has a simpler life, claiming that this "corresponds fairly well to our prereflective intuitions."[46] Tom Regan, on the other hand, after maintaining that the subjects-of-a-life, while having equal inherent value, can be differentially harmed by death, claims that "no reasonable person" would deny that the death of mentally more complex beings, which would be deprived of a greater range of opportunities for satisfaction[47], is a greater harm than the death of simpler beings.

These judgments clearly reintroduce the gradualist comparative criterion linked to mental complexity, without, however, appealing to Singer's method. How, then, are they founded? The first impression is that Rachels's reference to our prereflective intuitions, and Regan's criterion of the alleged opinion of any reasonable person, only repropose an identical, well known solution: the generic appeal to what people think. Were this the case, what we would face would be a foundation that, far from overcoming the problems of arbitrariness attendant on hypothetical choice, reintroduces them in a more severe form.

But no doubt what Rachels and Regan have in mind is not an appeal to current opinion but rather an implicit reference to something as straightforward as a mathematical calculation: the greater the complexity of the being, the greater the number of interests; the greater the number of interests, the greater the quantity of possible satisfaction; the greater the quantity of possible satisfaction, the greater the harm that the loss of life is.

Despite its seeming elegance, however, this solution has problems of its own. In estimating the opportunities for satisfaction, both Rachels and Regan focus once more on the structural characteristics of beings. In this perspective, the more autonomous, rational, communicative and so forth the being, the richer the possible prudential value of its existence. And yet, within a subjective approach, the merely quantitative calculation cannot be made *from outside*. The problem we have already confronted in the case of hypothetical choice reappears here in slightly different terms. If the value one wants to measure is prudential, its greater or lesser quantity can be measured from no viewpoint other than *that of the individual whose life is in question*. There is no "global" subject whose prudential value is made up of the net balance of the satisfaction and the frustration of all existing beings and from whose viewpoint it would make sense to evaluate harms by comparing the more of an individual with the less of another individual. But if, as a consequence of this, one is compelled to shift to an *internal* outlook for every existence in question, the quantitative evaluation of the harm's magnitude cannot but change radically.

Internal Perspectives on Prudential Value

At this point, there are two paths down which one can turn. The first leads to that egalitarian thesis about lives that Singer openly states he wants to avoid, and which always lurks behind subjective/quantitative theories.[48] Such a theory can be roughly summed up as follows. Intuitively, it appears plausible to grant differential value to lives. However, for each being, its own life is everything. In this sense, it is impossible to make comparisons: be it a child with Down's syndrome, a celebrated academic, a poor used-car salesman, or a dog, death means the end of everything. From the point of view of value, dying is something *categorical,* and therefore there are no greater or lesser levels of harm. Although theoretically plausible, the argument suffers from a severe fault for an action-guiding discipline such as ethics: by not providing any decision criterion for cases of conflict, it seems to be quite paralyzing on a practical level.

The second possibility is illustrated well by Evelyn Pluhar, who in a recent book has defended a deontological approach of Gewirthian descent. We will go back to Alan Gewirth's views in the next chapter. What interests us here is instead Pluhar's specific endeavor to provide a quantitative, but gradualist and noncategorical, internal account of the harm that death is. This endeavor consists in radically shifting attention from the structural capacities of beings—how much prudential value their lives can (allegedly) contain on the basis of the kinds of beings they are—to the aspects we have defined as accidental— how much prudential value their lives actually possess as against how much of it they might possess.[49] Pluhar argues that only by making this shift can one draw a comparison that is impartial in that it is guided by the very outlooks of the beings in question. And, in this perspective, the only factors that can be taken into consideration in assessing the harm that death is are those of a contingent sort, such as, for example, the foreseen length of individual existences and specific limits on welfare—limits that in extreme cases can reach the point of causing death to be a benefit rather than a harm, as it happens in the case of voluntary euthanasia.

One can clearly see here the difference between the outcomes of a subjective external account and those of a subjective internal account that seeks to remain gradualist. As against the external claim that "the more complex a being, the more objectionable its killing," the internal account asserts that there is no reason why the lives of the more complex beings should be more valuable than the lives of the simpler beings. And it goes further: it also makes it plausible to maintain that the harm that death is can be greater for the simpler beings in case the life of the more complex beings is affected by internal variables that reduce its prudential value—think of the choice between a cognitively simple but healthy and happy individual, and a cognitively complex but seriously and irredeemably suffering being.

It is obvious that, within this framework, the comparison between harms is not a comparison between integer quantities but between *fractional* quantities. In other words, the magnitude of every specific harm must be expressed in terms of the fractional subtraction from the overall welfare that is possible for a given kind of being. This holds both with respect to welfare and with respect to life expectancies. Suppose, for example, that we have to decide who is to be saved between a four-year-old child who suffers from an illness that will not allow him to reach puberty, and a perfectly healthy woman. The child might be expected to live about eight years more, and the woman might be expected to live about forty years more. On the face of it, it would seem plausible to say that it is the woman who would lose more by dying—a greater number of years of life. But the two integer quantities—eight years and forty years—do not account for the magnitude of the harm as seen from the *internal* perspective of the two beings involved. If, in fact, the time that is left to the woman is roughly analogous to that which she has already spent—it is, that is, the equivalent of half her life—the time that is left to the child is instead twice as much as the time he has already spent—it is, that is, the equivalent of two-thirds of his already short existence. It is therefore the child who must be saved, as it is the child who would be harmed to a greater extent by death.

This specific point allows us to return to the suggestion of DeGrazia that we previously set aside—the idea that welfare interests also have an instrumental value such that their frustration may be evaluated not only in itself but also in relation to the quantity of experiences that it precludes. DeGrazia draws from this the conclusion that the greater the mental complexity of a being, the greater the overall moral weight that should be afforded to its interests in welfare. But this conclusion only follows providing that one adopts the quantitative external approach based on integer quantities that the argument here developed with respect to the value of life has led us to exclude. If one shifts instead to the more tenable internal approach, given that the comparative evaluation of the foreclosed experiences is made on the basis of fractional quantities, the case for the comparative criterion of mental complexity loses its force. We can clarify this point with an example that concerns freedom, that is, the component of welfare in which, according to DeGrazia, instrumental value takes on the greatest weight. Think of a mentally fairly simple being—an elderly woman suffering from Alzheimer's disease. Suppose that her relatives, to avoid assuming too many responsibilities, restrict her freedom: for example, they prevent her from going out alone, even for a short time. As a consequence of this, the old woman suffers a direct loss—she does not like to be deprived of any freedom of movement—and an indirect loss—she cannot, let us say, have a short walk in the gardens in front of the house. Now, it is true that, if seen from an external perspective, what the old woman loses on the instrumental level may seem very little—on the face of it, watching children playing does not appear to be as worthwhile as listening to a classical music concert or giving a paper at a conference. And yet, if one takes the internal approach seriously, things change: if made proportionate to the pleasures that the rest of her life—given the kind of being that she is—offers to her, to sit in the park and watch the children may mean a great deal. The same can be said, obviously, of the limitation of freedom in the case of an intellectually unsophisticated nonhuman.

On the whole, then, a gradualist subjective/quantitative internal account appears not only to obviate many of the problems that the other views on the value of life run into but to shed light on questions about welfare as well. Not even this approach, however, is exempt from difficulties. First and foremost, there is a problem of fairness. For if it is true that the levels of satisfaction and frustration that characterize individual existences are mostly due to chance—think of illness, accidents, or even socioeconomic conditions—granting lesser value to the life of a being on the basis of such factors, except for the case in which life has become intolerable, seems at the least morally arbitrary.[50] And second, if one takes seriously the problem of comparisons, the distance from the egalitarian thesis about lives is not so great as to entirely eliminate the risk of an impasse at the practical level.

An Open Problem

It is worthwhile to summarize the results we have reached thus far. Concerning welfare, it seems that the presumption in favor of equal consideration, with the attendant elimination of all comparative criteria in favor of the simple maintenance of the inclusive criterion of consciousness, can hardly be reversed. On the one hand, deontological approaches, which mark a sharp leap in status by the immediate appeal to one or more psychological characteristics, do not comply with the prerequisite of contextual relevance. On the other, the mediate appeal to mental complexity in connection with the instrumental aspect of the value of welfare seems to run into the same difficulties as the analogous appeal in the case of life: untenable on the basis of an external perspective, it becomes empty if one adopts an internal perspective.

As for the protection of life, the situation can be summarized more or less as follows. The approach that attributes an immediate role to self-consciousness appears problematic by reason of its refusal to see in the harm that death is the aspect of deprivation as well as that of infliction. This seems to exclude the comparative criterion of self-consciousness. The appeal to the possession of a specific characteristic, or to mental complexity, if inserted within the framework of the subjective/qualitative approach is wanting on the level of justification, and, if inserted within the framework of the objective/qualitative approach, seems objectionable because of its (more or less open) reference to a metaphysical background. The comparative criterion of mental complexity seems instead more plausible when introduced into a subjective/quantitative framework. Among the subjective/quantitative solutions resting on an external perspective, however, the view appealing to hypothetical choice suffers from problems of implementability both at the imaginative and at the theoretical level, and the view appealing to mathematical calculation rests on a fallacy. If, on the other hand, one turns to the subjective/quantitative solutions resting on an internal perspective, the egalitarian thesis about lives, with its categorical account and its maintenance of the single criterion of consciousness, appears paralyzing, and the proportional quantitative approach is difficult to apply and tends to embody arbitrary elements.

The general situation as regards possible comparative criteria is therefore rather more complicated than it might appear. The review of the problems involved, brief as it has been, shows how much preliminary work is still needed in order to formulate a rationally acceptable theory of overall moral status. In the next chapter, I will argue for an approach that seems to me to be a first theoretical/practical step in this direction. But, perhaps, a reflection on the concept of person may still help us shed some light on the matter.

The Notion of Person as an Alternative Solution?

In a recent article, David DeGrazia launches a strong attack on the notion of person. The piece is occasioned by the publication of a collection of readings in which several authors argue for the attribution of personhood to the nonhuman great apes, employing such a move as a starting point to demand a radical change in their ethical treatment.[51] DeGrazia's criticisms can thus be a useful guide for an analysis aimed at determining whether the concept of person can shed some light on the problem of possible levels within moral status.

It is worth first quickly illustrating the essays in question. The shared reference point is Daniel Dennett's well known analysis according to which being a person requires the following: being rational, being intentional, and being perceived as rational and intentional; reciprocating by perceiving others as rational and intentional; and, finally, being capable of verbal communication and of self-consciousness.[52] Since, as Dennett himself acknowledges, most intelligent beings display the possession of the first four requisites, the discussion tends to focus on the linguistic capacity and on the capacity for self-consciousness. Having dealt elsewhere with the question of verbal communication, here I will summarize only the aspects that concern the latter capacity—aspects that are sometimes intertwined with the very sensible use of sign language.

According to a well-established account, there exist at least three levels of self-awareness, usually described as basic self-awareness, perspective self-awareness, and reflective self-awareness. Undoubtedly, a basic form of self-awareness is a prerequisite for the use of personal pronouns and self-referents. Like human children, signing individuals among the nonhuman great apes begin using them at the same time that they begin passing the famous test of self-recognition in mirrors. Forms of perspective self-awareness are implied both by the ability to talk about oneself in situations removed in space and time, which can be found in all the great apes instructed in sign language, and by the capacity to formulate and carry out even complex plans—for example, cooperation schemes—extensively present in free-living individuals. Finally, reflexive self-consciousness is in its turn a composite capacity. The first level consists of the presence of a "theory of mind," that is, of the ability to attribute mental states to other beings. Such a faculty, which enables one to go beyond a purely egocentric outlook in order to assume the other's perspective, is easily detectable in the great apes, for example, by virtue of the phenomenon of intentional deception, which, as we have already noticed, requires the capacity to see events from the viewpoint of the interlocutor, negating her perception. The higher level implies instead the ability to recognize that the other recognizes that we have a mind—it implies, that is, the attribution of a theory of mind to the other. This level too has been observed in the nonhuman great apes, in particular through cases of "deception of the deceiver."[53]

These and other similar data are impressive and DeGrazia neither denies them nor plays down their significance. His strategy lies instead in employing the appeal to intuitions as a ground for claiming that the concept of person is not able to decide cases of such a kind. And this is because, in his view, the notion of "person" is (a) unanalyzable, insofar as it points at a generic set of characteristics (the reference is here to the Wittgensteinian idea of "cluster concept") rather than to a set of necessary and sufficient conditions; (b) not determinate but vague, since each of these characteristics is multidimensional and gradational; and (c) descriptively redundant, because the assertion that X is a person adds no descriptive content to the assertion that X has the characteristics in question.[54] On this perspective, the conclusion DeGrazia reaches is that we should drop the concept of personhood except where who counts as a person is not in question, since only in such situations a "rhetorical" use of the term would be useful, or at least innocuous. We should, for example, remind jingoistic Americans that Iraqis are persons, because "here persons are just humans, where the assumption is that they have full moral status"; but we should not appeal to personhood when it comes to nonhumans such as the great apes, or dolphins.[55]

First of all, what is one to say about the appeal to intuitions? The reference to the intuitive aspect of the concept is relatively common: many of the authors who write on the subject refer to the characteristics that come to mind when we hear or use the word "person," or invite us to not stray too much from what people think when they employ the notion. But is it plausible to maintain that such appeal is the only viable solution as far as the concept of person is concerned? Apparently not. For there exists a different, and perhaps sounder, alternative, which lies in making reference to the philosophical, rather than to the current, usage of the term. As has been asserted on the subject of rights, in the case of "person," too, what we are dealing with is a creature of ethical theories, and so it is to ethical theories that we must look if we are to understand its meaning.[56]

Besides reducing the risk, peculiar to the reference to intuitions, of an uncritical assumption of prejudices, the alternative of the reference to the philosophical usage helps to prevent that fragmentation of the concept that can result from trying to accommodate disparate material. We will thus try to briefly reexamine the question starting not from what people think but rather from the less hazy analysis of the philosophical roots of "person."

We have already noticed that the notion of person and the notion of human being, though they are still currently used as if they had the same meaning, tend to be no longer seen as equivalent in bioethical discussions, and that many authors, after drawing a distinction between the biological and the philosophical sense of human being, have opted for using only for the latter, and not for the former, the term "person." The insistence on this distinction is fully consistent with the history of the concept, whose use in connection with God within the context of the Christian theological controversies about the dogma of the Trinity prevented it from the beginning from simply becoming another term for "human being." In this light, it is possible to claim that the element of species-neutrality that has recently been claimed for it is in fact a constituent aspect of the notion. DeGrazia agrees on this point, arguing for his part that "person" cannot mean "human being," not only because some members of our species are not persons but also "for . . . the reason that some logically possible— and perhaps some actual—persons are not humans."[57] And yet, as we have seen, he concludes that we cannot assert that (at least some) actually existing nonhuman animals fall within this category. Why?

His argument, which ensues from the first two criticisms of the notion, can be summarized as follows: since what our intuition point at in the case of "person" is an imprecise set of properties, and since there are different kinds of these properties and each kind comes in degrees, the notion is neither clearly nor nonarbitrarily applicable— and thus is morally unhelpful—in contexts in which who qualifies as a person is "genuinely debatable."[58]

And yet, when it was introduced into philosophical jargon by the Stoics, the Latin term "person," which initially meant a mask worn by an actor in classical drama, and consequently the character the actor performed, fulfilled a relatively clear function—it indicated, that is, the role one is called to play in life. Both the idea of a role and the reference to a task to be accomplished seem to point at an interpretation of the concept of person in terms of a *subject of relations*. Given the prominence of the notion of relation in premodern ethics from Aristotle at least up to classical natural law, it is on the whole plausible to hold that the appeal to the capacity for reasoning that was later to appear in many authors is but a derivative element as compared to this more basic aspect.[59]

Historically, such an aspect has appeared in the shape both of self-relation (self-consciousness) and of heterorelation (relationships with others). Though self-relation has gradually acquired supremacy, heterorelation cannot be immediately dismissed. Apart from being more faithful to the original meaning of the word, with its reference to a role to play, the latter is the only sense in which the concept of person can be meaningfully contrasted—as it so frequently was in moral philosophy—with the concept of "thing." Since thing is an older and more widespread notion than person, the more sensible procedure is to get going from it, and not the other way round; and the determinative conditions of application of the concept of thing have generally to do with passiveness and unawareness. Such a reading raises the question whether one may not in the end interpret the notion of "person" in terms of the simple possibility of relating to other beings and, consequently, of the mere capacity for consciousness. The suggestion is less eccentric than one may think: not only one can find traces of it at least in the Stoics but the already mentioned neo-Kantian philosopher Leonard Nelson, at the beginning of the twentieth century, and—with different levels of articulation—P. F. Strawson and Steve Sapontzis, more recently, put forward this view.[60]

As for the aspect of self-relation, on the other hand, it becomes particularly prominent starting from the moment when the concept of person tends to be identified with subjective identity, that is, with the unity and continuity of the conscious life of the self. Locke defines a person as "a thinking intelligent being that has reason and reflection and can consider itself as itself, the same thinking thing, in different times and places,"[61] and even Kant, with all his insistence on rationality, claims that it is the fact of being able to represent to themselves their own selves that elevates persons above other beings.[62] Within this framework, the capacity to have an enduring concept of one's self appears in some way connected with the idea of a complex subjectivity, capable of reasoning and of assuming responsibility.

On the basis of this quick reconstruction, then, the concept of person does not prove to be unanalyzable, insofar as it revolves around key-properties that are clearly identifiable thanks to the guide lent by the notion of relation. As for the charge of vagueness, it too appears difficult to uphold. For if it is true that the key-properties are multidimensional and gradational, as we saw with reference to self-consciousness, all that is needed is a stipulation as to the required level—a stipulation that DeGrazia himself accepts when he claims that there are situations where "who counts as a person is not in question." From this it seems to follow that the concept of person can be sensibly applied—subject to a decision about its specific interpretation and the specific threshold required—to all individuals, human and nonhuman, in which the key-properties can be detected.

If, therefore, as it seems, chimpanzees, gorillas, and orangutans are not only conscious but also suitably self-conscious, there are no particular hindrances to including them among persons. (Incidentally, it is interesting to note that the first of Dennett's basic requirements is self-consciousness, and that the second, that is, the use of language, is a particularly demanding interpretation of communicative ability and thus of the capacity for heterorelations). Although this contradicts the thesis that we should use the notion only when "who counts as a person is not in question," the soundness of this conclusion is confirmed by the historical vicissitudes of the concept, marked as they are by a gradual extension to beings previously seen as borderline cases, such as women and slaves. All this seems to show that the rhetorical usage of "person," far from being useful only when it comes to strengthening the paradigm, turns out to be particularly valuable in just those cases in which moral reform is at stake.[63]

The situation is different with the idea that the concept may be descriptively redundant. To consider this point, it may be useful to remember that philosophical discussions of "person" often emphasized that the term is employed in two ways. In brief, to say of a being that it is a person in the *descriptive* sense is to convey some information about what the being is like, and this can amount to saying that it has some specific characteristics; but to use the term in a *normative* way is to use it to ascribe moral properties to the being so denominated—usually some rights or duties, and frequently the right to life, as is well illustrated by a recent definition according to which a person is an entity that possesses at least one of the permanent, nonpotential properties that make it intrinsically wrong to destroy it.[64]

DeGrazia denies that the notion of person can be used in a purely prescriptive way. He argues that it is a *hybrid* notion—partly informative and partly evaluative—in which the concept adds to the descriptive content connected with the favored properties a judgment about the moral status of the beings that possess the properties. This is in agreement with the line of interpretation so far followed, which suggests that the normative power of the concept originates in the reference to properties connected with a value-laden notion such as that of relation, and that accordingly, far from existing independently, the prescriptive and the descriptive aspects are "two different and unstable resting points on the same continuum."[65]

That the prescriptive aspect cannot be considered as quite redundant seems to be demonstrated by the very usage of the notion in view of ethical change—a usage that displays, as Harlan B. Miller has observed, a significant action-guiding power.[66] What instead about the view that the possibility of directly appealing to the relevant properties makes the descriptive aspect redundant? On the basis of the philosophical history of "person," we have so far reached the conclusion that, if construed in terms of heterorelation, the concept points at the possession of consciousness, and if construed in terms of self-relation, it points instead at the possession of self-consciousness. But, on one hand, consciousness is nothing other than the inclusive criterion of moral status adopted by the great majority of authors. And, on the other, self-consciousness, if understood in a specific sense,[67] exactly coincides with one of the comparative criteria that we have seen play a role in the debate on the value of life and, if understood in a more generic sense, appears to point instead at another of these criteria—namely, mental complexity.

It seems therefore that, on the whole, notwithstanding the divergence with respect to the interpretation and to the possibilities for application of the concept, the view we have at this point developed did not lead us far from DeGrazia's conclusions on the redundancy of its descriptive content. For if one considers this aspect, our reflection on the notion of person seems to have provided us neither with a new approach nor with any contents that aren't already present in the accounts that directly appeal to relevant characteristics.[68] But if this is the case, it is clear that, far from resolving them, the concept of person simply reintroduces in other terms the problems about moral status that we have thus far run into.

Chapter 6

■■

A Minimal Normative Proposal

In a variegated world, inhabited by diverse vulnerable and competing beings, in a reality where to unavoidable conflicts are added conflicts caused by the idea that might is right, what could be the minimal cohabitation rules, and to whom should they apply?

To this question, as far as the members of our species are concerned, we have endeavored to give an answer. It is the idea of human rights. In this last chapter I will examine the premises and implications of the doctrine of human rights as it has gradually been elaborated and publicly established. In so doing, I will consider the way this doctrine has tried to overcome at least the most serious among the difficulties highlighted by the analysis thus far developed, and I will examine the possibility that its theoretical foundations offer a suitable solution for the problems of a community broader than the human one. In other words, I will try to ascertain whether human rights theory can be a plausible preliminary answer also for cohabitation with the members of other species.

Human Rights: Sphere of Reference

Human rights do not cover the whole of morality. It can be plausibly claimed, in fact, that they have to do with that more limited theory of conduct which, when dealing with the question of moral status, we defined as "morality in the narrow sense." The notion, traditionally ascribed to G. J. Warnock, was taken up among others by J. L. Mackie, who explained it in terms of a particular sort of constraints whose central task is to set limits to the individuals' pursuit of their own selfish goals. In this sense, one may say that it finds a parallel in the Strawsonian notion of "social morality"—of a morality, that is, which is not about diversity of kinds of life but about uniformity of practices. The content of narrow morality hence pertains to the realm of the *right,* not to that of the *good;* to the domain of the obligatory, not of the supererogatory. More precisely, it refers to a limited subset of the principles that make up the sphere of the right.[1]

As I have suggested, one might be tempted to identify narrow morality with deontological constraints as opposed to consequentialist prescriptions. Some authors have done something of the kind. But, on the one hand, there are deontological prescriptions that are not included in narrow morality—for example, the rule against lying. On the other, there are consequentialist defenses of the limits that narrow morality imposes. The well known "harm principle," whose first formulation is Bentham's but whose most detailed defense is Mill's, states for example that the only purpose for which power can be rightfully exercised over any member of a community against her will is to prevent harm to others.[2] Even if this principle, in not focusing only on basic harms, does not exactly coincide with the scope of narrow morality, its rationale is exactly that of erecting a sort of barrier around the individual.

That said, one must acknowledge that the prescriptions of narrow morality seem better secured in a deontological context, which can produce (nearly) absolute constraints. In everyday morality, this criterion of near-absoluteness, which implies an argumentative threshold and an almost unconditional exclusion of trade-offs between values, has naturally been translated into the language of rights. The same thing tends to occur at a more theoretical level. As Joseph Raz argues, rights generally do exactly what narrow morality is supposed to do and thus,

> on the plausible assumption that the only valid grounds on which the free pursuit by people of their own lives can be restricted are the needs, interests, and preferences of other people it becomes plausible to regard (narrow) morality as right-based.[3]

In this light, human rights doctrine seems to have the function of, and to be particularly suited to, meeting a special class of moral concerns: those which, having to do with the basic protection of individuals, appear to be not only the most important, but also the most sharable and the most independent of specific spatial and temporal contexts.

It might be objected that such an interpretation, laying stress essentially on *noninterference,* points toward an unjustifiedly minimalist account of human rights. After all, the modern conception has gradually added a new side to the doctrine, in particular in the form of welfare rights or social and economic rights. Yet it is plausible to maintain that the core of the theory remains protective, and that between the two main sorts of rights—*negative* rights, or rights not to be treated in a certain way, and *positive* rights, or rights to be treated in a certain way[4]—the ones that prevail are always negative rights, and, in particular, the so-called civil liberties, secured by the generalized prohibition against taking life, depriving of freedom, and violating bodily integrity. Apart from the widely accepted ethical priority of nonmaleficence over beneficence, it is clear that there are serious pragmatic reasons for this emphasis. Negative rights, being less affected by conditions of scarcity, are less likely to be subject to exceptions and thus offer the significant advantage of being more easily implementable.

However, negative rights too imply a positive aspect. Onora O'Neill, working within a Kantian framework and using the language of duties, has stressed that principles that prescribe rejection of fundamental harm do not establish the basic obligation not to cause harm, but rather the basic obligation to prevent the harms in question— that is to say, the obligation not to make harm a constitutive principle of lives and institutions. Effective limitation of harm can thus demand selective harm in self-defense and for the defense of others, as well as the creation of political and legal institutions that coerce in order to secure such limitation.[5] This aspect becomes even more relevant once translated into the language of rights, because if focusing on duties and on their possible infringement gives center stage to the moral agent, rights adopt instead the perspective of the moral patient, and hence of the possible victim of harm. Thus, to uphold fundamental negative rights does not mean to accept not to infringe such rights, but rather to uphold the construction of a social order that embodies them and takes charge of their implementation and protection.

In this sense, human rights, while being claimed as moral rights, are also proposed as legal rights.[6] And although the status within international law of the declarations and conventions approved by the United Nations General Assembly is a complex question, the rights that are there asserted have strong legal overtones. This implies that the use of force can be justified in securing them.

Human Rights: Essential Characteristics

> We hold these truths to be self-evident: That all men [*sic*] are created equal; that they are endowed by their Creator with certain unalienable rights; that among these are life, liberty, and the pursuit of happiness; that, to secure these rights, governments are instituted . . .

This is what the Declaration of Independence of the United States proclaims. And, thirteen years later, the Declaration of the Rights of Man [*sic*] and of the Citizen thus echoes it:

> Men are born and remain free and equal in rights. . . . The aim of all political association is the preservation of the natural and imprescriptible rights of man. These rights are liberty, property, security, and resistance to oppression.

Much has been written on the difficulties raised by the foundation of the so-called "rights of man." The American Declaration epistemologically has recourse to self-evidence, and on the foundational level appeals to God. What about the French Declaration? The boldness with which it forgoes all justification was already underlined by Bentham, who, after describing natural rights as "nonsense," dismissed natural and imprescriptible rights as "nonsense upon stilts."[7] Concerning the notion of right, however, Bentham was far from being an impartial judge. Actually, behind the two declarations one can detect, more or less distinctly, the powerful tradition of natural rights, in which self-evidence is warranted by a reason assumed to be common to all human beings, God's law is at the same time the law of nature, and rights are inalienable "moral qualities" of individuals. Contractarian approaches add to this the idea that civil society originates in an agreement whose aim is to better preserve these natural rights.

In the transition from the doctrine of natural rights to the doctrine of human rights, the main attending changes concern just such foundational aspects, which are therefore deserving of a separate discussion. What is worth stressing in this context is instead the fact that each Declaration establishes a close connection between rights and governments or political associations. Natural rights underlie civil rights, and existing or in-the-making societies are bound first to acknowledge them and then to safeguard them. The call for an implementation of narrow morality thus takes the form of a request for the acknowledgment of preexisting moral properties directed *at institutions*.

From the beginning, therefore, the so-called "rights of man" have an eminently political character. As Margaret MacDonald observes in a pioneering article on the subject, they were not conceived in order to be enjoyed on a desert island but in order to become "clauses in Constitutions, the inspiration of social and governmental reforms."[8] This element is only apparently in contrast to the definition of "natural" rights, which suggests an existence independent of organized society. For apart from the obvious role played by the specific philosophical framework I have just mentioned, the attribute "natural" emphasizes in a right its *basic* character. And this in two senses. On the one hand, to say of a right that it is "natural" somehow implies the idea that it is unacquired—that it does not arise from special circumstances, like particular transactions between individuals or particular positions within the community—and that it cannot therefore be lost as a consequence of changes in one's individual condition or in the general context.[9] On the other hand, although the injunction to keep promises or the exhortation to be beneficent are not very likely to be inserted among the watchwords of reformers or demonstrators, issues like the protection of life, of freedom, and of security are fundamental moral values that must be realized in any acceptable society.

Such an eminently political aspect persists, and is even heightened, in human rights doctrine. In this context, too, the basic idea is that responsibility for implementation lies primarily with institutions. And the first requirement for this is obviously that infringements of rights not be sanctioned by the society's legal system. It was through a concern of this sort that the drafters of the United Nations Declaration of 1948 felt the need, for example, to insert an article that explicitly forbids any form of slavery, servitude, and slave trade.[10] *Codified* killing, confinement, mutilation and torture are just the opposite of the protection of the life, freedom, and bodily integrity of the community's members. As has been noticed, in this sense the internal sovereignty of states is limited, and one of the functions of human rights is exactly that of defining the limits of such sovereignty.[11]

It is worth dwelling upon this point. I have already observed that the return to the Enlightenment tradition of natural rights that led to the formulation of human rights doctrine was prompted by the need to check those forms of institutionalized violence and discrimination that had marked the first half of the twentieth century. It was to that idea of the inalienable value of the individual which in the age of the great revolutions had undertaken the function of limiting organized power that it was natural to turn after the horrors of the Third Reich. As Catharine MacKinnon puts it:

> This organized genocide by government policy indelibly marked and fundamentally shaped the content, priorities, sensitivities, and deep structure of the received law of human rights in our time. In a reading of this reality, more than any other, contemporary human rights finds its principled ground.[12]

In this perspective, it is plausible to assert that the model of violation of human rights is based on the organization and action of the state.

Recently, such institutional reading has been the object of an interesting reelaboration by the American philosopher Thomas Pogge.[13] By postulating an individual P's right to X as a human right, Pogge claims, what we are asserting is "that P's society ought to be (re)organized in such a way that P has secure access to X and, in particular, so that P is secure against being denied X or deprived of X officially."[14] On the basis of an analysis of the structural characteristics of human rights as they have historically evolved starting from the earlier doctrine of natural rights, Pogge argues, like MacKinnon, that disrespect for human rights is paradigmatically exemplified by government violations—violations that may take the form of the creation or maintenance of unjust laws, or even of a perverse construction of neutral laws. Inversely, therefore, the flourishing of human rights depends in the first instance on a society's institutions—on its constitution and its laws.

On the whole, thus, it seems that violations of human rights, to count as such, must be in a sense official, and that, accordingly, human rights protect individuals only against violations from particular sources. These sources can be legal systems, governments and their representatives, armed forces, and in general any institutional body—but not individual members of the community. Following Pogge again, such an idea can be concisely captured by conceiving it to be implicit in the notion of human rights that the prescriptions that such rights imply are addressed, at least primarily, to those who hold positions of authority within a state or another comparable social system.

Human Rights: Justification

The impossibility of making reference to the intentions of a divine creator, and the wish to avoid the metaphysical connotations of the idea of natural law, are among the main reasons why, gradually, the language of natural rights was replaced by the new language of human rights. Thus, while natural rights theory, as we have seen, claims not only that human beings ("men") have certain rights but also that these rights have distinct epistemic properties and a specific ontological status, human rights theory is neutral as far as epistemology and ontology are concerned.[15] Human rights simply are a particular, and particularly important, subset of moral rights in a broad sense. While not emerging in the Universal Declaration of 1948—which, after stating that all human beings "are born free and equal in dignity and rights," confines itself to adding that "they are endowed with reason and conscience and should act towards one another in a spirit of brotherhood"[16]—this aspect is made clear by the theoretical elaboration carried out in the years following its promulgation.

Owing to the neutrality of human rights doctrine, there is the possibility of alternative approaches to the problem of justification. Since, unlike the public at large and the drafters of political manifestoes, philosophers must offer reasons for the views they put forward, in the case in question they must explain the *why* of human rights—that is to say, they must explain what it is that, in human beings, justifies the equal attribution of the particular sort of moral claims grouped together under the label of "human rights."

We know that it cannot be the mere fact of being human in the sense of being a member of *Homo sapiens*, because species membership in itself has no moral relevance. Most of the philosophers who confront the question seem to be somehow aware of this problem. When it is bestowed a role, in fact, reference to species is introduced in a hurried and oblique way. For example, Hugo Adam Bedau writes:

> Are human rights to be thought of as possessed by all and only persons, human beings, or human persons? On the first alternative, some animals . . . might turn out to have human rights. On the last alternative, human fetuses and severely retarded adults might lack human rights. On the middle alternative neither of these results is likely to occur, and so it is the least controversial way to resolve the problem. The concept of human rights was not designed to embrace non-human persons, and it was clearly intended to exclude infra-human beings, such as animals.[17]

It is even possible that the justificatory aspect is simply evaded. This is the case with, among others, A. I. Melden:

> Instead of looking for a basis for human rights, we need to see more clearly and in its rich and complex detail just what it is for persons to have the rights they have as human beings. It is here that all explanations come to an end.[18]

If one thinks that what is at stake is the maximum level of moral status, positions of this sort do appear philosophically hasty.

There are, however, perspectives in which the appeal to species membership clearly performs a subsidiary and, so to speak, rhetorical function. It is in such instances that the search for a justification for human rights moves in a theoretically fertile direction. It is in particular the American philosopher Gregory Vlastos who is to be credited with pointing out this direction from the dawn of contemporary debate.[19] While still expressing himself in terms of persons or human beings (notions he uses interchangeably), Vlastos—who discusses justice and equality—does not hesitate to set aside the biological element in favor of a direct appeal to psychological characteristics. One might think that what will come to the fore is what we have defined as the philosophical sense of "human being," that is, the reference to capacities like rationality and self-consciousness, usually connected with the concept of person. But this is not how things stand. Vlastos begins by arguing that only valuers do not need to be valued by others in order to have value. For they attribute value to themselves and, in particular, (a) to the fact of having positive conscious experiences and (b) to the fact of making one's own choices—bringing under this term not only deliberate decisions but also "those subtler modulations and more spontaneous expressions of individual preference which could scarcely be called 'choices' or 'decisions.'"[20] The next step is that of translating the idea of equal human value ("worth"), which in a more or less explicit way underlies human rights doctrine, into the idea of the equal value of human well-being and freedom.[21] And this is because, Vlastos argues, in all cases where human beings are capable of enjoying the same goods—the example offered is relief from acute physical pain—the intrinsic value of their enjoyment is the same; and because choosing for oneself has the same intrinsic value for all individuals, independently of what they happen to choose. The conclusion is that the attribution of equal value to individual welfare and freedom is the ground for the attribution of equal (prima facie) rights to welfare and freedom.

If one examines Vlastos's account ignoring the humanist bias, what one confronts is a subjective-quantitative approach based on an internal perspective. On the one hand, in fact, the use of the term "intrinsic," far from pointing at questionable metaphysical claims, refers here merely to the contrast between *prudential* value and the value *for others* of the experiences of welfare and freedom. If X were a statesman, Vlastos explains, and giving him relief from pain enabled him to benefit millions of individuals, and if Y, in contrast, were an unskilled laborer, who would be the sole beneficiary of the like relief, we would of course agree that the extrinsic value of the two experiences would be greatly different—but not their intrinsic value.[22] On the other hand, only an approach that excludes alleged objective frameworks and qualitative evaluations, and that adopts an internal outlook can yield the egalitarian outcomes that Vlastos reaches—outcomes that are avowedly at odds with the perfectionist principle that the greater the psychological complexity of a being, the greater the moral weight to be afforded to its interests:

> [N]o matter how A and B might differ in taste and style of life, they would both crave relief from acute physical pain. In that case, we would put the same value on giving this to either of them, regardless of the fact that A might be a talented, brilliantly successful person, B "a mere nobody."[23]

As I have pointed out, there are several views that, as regards the interests in freedom and welfare, defend equal consideration. What differentiates Vlastos's account is, however, that it roots *the equal value of individuals* precisely in the equal value of the two prudential elements considered as basic—in the experience, that is, of freedom and welfare. This has fundamental implications for the problem of the value of life. For it is a necessary, though not declared, implication of this account that the right to life ensues from the fact that continued existence is a prerequisite for enjoying the rights to welfare and freedom. But if being alive is the necessary requirement for benefiting by welfare and freedom, the right to life is rooted in the instrumental value of existence. On the one hand, this rules out the appeal to the possession of the desire to go on living, or of the ability to value life, as prerequisites for such right, in clear contrast with the positions that draw a line between beings that are able, and beings that are not able, to conceive of themselves as entities endowed with a past and a future. And on the other, a value that is instrumental with respect to goods that have equal intrinsic value cannot but be equal, with the consequence that the right to life cannot vary in strength according to the structural capacities of the being. Even concerning the question of the value of life, therefore, the doctrine of human rights as it is outlined by Vlastos proves to be radically egalitarian.

Vlastos's reference to the capacity to enjoy welfare and the fact of making one's own choices generates a line of defense of human rights that will be found again in Alan Gewirth, after going through intermediate historical/theoretical stages. Among these, the most important one is perhaps the already cited essay on racial discrimination by Richard Wasserstrom.[24] After reconsidering Vlastos's argument, which he explicitly draws on, Wasserstrom introduces at least two novel elements. The first concerns the grounds for the centrality of freedom and welfare. After stressing that the presence of rights enhances the moral landscape just in that it makes it possible to focus on the being which is adversely affected by the action, that is, on the being which suffers the injury, Wasserstrom argues that freedom and welfare must be protected by fundamental rights because the denial of the opportunity to enjoy these rights prevents any possibility of developing one's capabilities and of living a satisfying life:

> Hence, to take one thing that is a precondition of well-being, the relief from acute physical pain, this is the kind of enjoyment that ought to be protected as a right of some kind just because without such relief there is precious little that one can effectively do or become.[25]

This reference to the active side of the subject, to what it can do or become, points at a path that will turn out to be fruitful.

The second element relates instead to Vlastos's egalitarian conclusion. Wasserstrom holds that the claim that the enjoyment drawn from the same fundamental goods is the same for every subject is inadequately defended. Thus, he aks himself afresh the question why the intrinsic value of the fruition of welfare and freedom should be considered equal for all individuals, and, after considering other hypotheses, ends up by resorting to a dual argument. Basically, his answer is that either individuals are in fact equally capable of enjoying these goods, and thus the values in question are actually equal for all, or, if there are differences, they are not in principle discoverable or measurable, and therefore we should opt anyway for equality, insofar as the opposite choice can result in precluding the possibility of living a satisfying life.[26]

In this way, although taking a more convoluted route that involves the introduction of the benefit of the doubt, Wasserstrom not only does not abandon the appeal to the capacity to attribute value to welfare and freedom introduced by Vlastos, but he comes to practically equivalent conclusions about the *equality* of the rights meant to protect such fundamental goods. References to the alleged exclusive humanness of these rights sound thus all the more superfluous and arbitrary—actually reaching explicit paradox with the assertion that the enjoyment of goods like relief from acute physical pain "in a real sense . . . differentiates human from nonhuman entities."[27]

As we have already noticed, similar elements of inadequacy with respect to the question of species are present in Alan Gewirth—recall his statement that "for human rights to be had, one must only be human." And yet, in his instance even more than in the previous ones, this is merely a matter of superstructure. In its most abstract form, Gewirth's argument is in fact an elaboration on the theme of the golden rule, and points therefore in the direction of the formal core of ethics.[28]

Starting from the idea that all moral codes are guides for action, Gewirth develops an argument that revolves around the concept of agent, construed as an intentional (that is, a conscious and purposive) being that wants to achieve its goals. To determine which moral code to follow, Gewirth argues, we need in the first instance to ask ourselves what is necessary for action itself. As reflective agents, we understand that the preconditions for agency are the capacity to have goals and the possibility of pursuing them. The capacity to have goals, which lies at what we have called the structural level, is conditional on the presence of minimal mental and physical abilities. The possibility of pursuing such goals, which lies instead at the accidental level, requires on the one hand absence of coercion, or freedom, and on the other a quality of life that affords a certain degree of security and opportunities and that can be recapitulated as welfare. But, Gewirth observes, if freedom and welfare are needed by agents to pursue their goals, all reflective agents advance, at least implicitly, a claim to such goods. In other words, every agent is logically compelled by the mere fact of engaging in action to accept evaluative judgments about the positivity of her possession of freedom and welfare, and deontic judgments about her rights to freedom and welfare. It is clear that, in this phase, such rights—which Gewirth calls "generic"—are not yet characterized as moral rights but appear only in the form of normative claims justified in prudential terms.[29]

The next step in the argument is the transition from being a mere reflective agent, who considers only her own interests, to being an agent who takes into account the interests of others as well. In the first place, Gewirth states, the reflective agent realizes that the reason which justifies her claim to the generic rights lies *only in being an agent,* since the appeal to any other characteristic, including that of being a reflective agent, would lead her to contradict herself through implying that, were she devoid of that characteristic, she would not possess the rights in question. In the second place, once she has identified in agency the relevant similarity between herself and her possible recipients, the reflective agent understands that the application of the principle of universalizability to this judgment logically entails the generalization that the rights she claims for herself belong to all agents.[30] This determines the transition from the prudential to the moral, and the rights in question turn into moral rights. This is, put most simply, the argument for what Gewirth defines as the Principle of Generic Consistency: "Act in accord with the generic rights of your recipients as well as of yourself."[31] It is evident that such a principle is nothing but a version of the formal principle of consistency, according to which like cases should be treated alike. With a difference, however. For if the traditional principle leaves unspecified both the moral prescriptions and the definition of the relevant similarity, in the case of Gewirth's principle the theoretical centrality of action determines both the prescriptive content—the rights to the preconditions of action—and the criterion of similarity—the fact of being an agent.

Owing also to its avowed aim of developing an overall theory of morality capable of regulating, in addition to relationships between individuals and organized power, individual transactions as well,

Gewirth's account is the most structured version of the line of argument connecting human rights with the protection of interests in freedom and welfare. The focus on the abstract notion of agent not only does away with any—even purely denominative—reference to species membership but retains the stress on the subject's evaluative side present in Vlastos, while at the same time elaborating on the appeal to the subject's active side that appears in Wasserstrom. The criterion of the capacity to enjoy freedom and welfare remains central, though no longer directly but rather instrumentally with respect to action. And, since these constituents come into play at the formal level, as prerequisites needed by the agents in order to be able to enjoy the categorical good that the pursuit of their own goals is, their comparative value should not even be measured, but is equal *ex hypothesi*. The same can be said with respect to life, whose role of a precondition for freedom and welfare is finally made explicit.[32] The result is a view that grants equal rights to freedom, welfare, and life to whoever is an agent, once again barring the way to those forms of perfectionism that award moral advantages on the basis of mental complexity.

For an Expanded Theory of Human Rights

We may briefly summarize the discussion thus far as follows. Human rights tend to cover the domain of morality in the narrow sense and are therefore essentially negative rights, or rights to noninterference. They are, moreover, institutional in character, in the sense that the model of both their implementation and their violation is based on the organization and the action of the state.

Within the moral community, human rights define the sphere of beings endowed with full moral status and, on the basis of their most convincing line of defense, the comparative criterion for access to such sphere is simply the fact of being an agent, that is, the fact of being an intentional being that has goals and wants to achieve them. This means that neither rationality nor any other among the cognitive qualities traditionally considered as "superior" is required. This plausible theoretical aspect, which meets among other things the felt need to eliminate any possible form of discrimination connected with what Richard Hare has defined as "ideals,"[33] that is, with specific hierarchical worldviews, is paralleled by the social fact that human rights, and the protection stemming from them, are seen as a prerogative of all intentional members of our species, whatever the psychological differences between them. Given that the beings that fulfill the requisite of intentionality are characterized by the capacity to enjoy freedom and welfare, as well as life which is a precondition for them, both directly and as prerequisites for action, the specific rights claimed concern freedom, welfare, and life. Such rights are equal for all their holders, because the value of the goods they protect is equal, and, as a consequence of this, the sphere characterized by full moral status is homogenous rather than stratified.

Is the comparative criterion of the possession of intentionality—undoubtedly general, connected with empirical properties, and morally relevant—able to stand the test of contextual relevance? The answer to this question depends on the kind of difference in treatment it can mark with respect to beings debarred from full moral status. At present, for the doctrine of human rights, the treatment of beings that seem to meet only the inclusive criterion of consciousness is, as shown by the issue of abortion, an open question that fluctuates between the mere prohibition of cruelty and some forms of graduated protection for life. It is clear that, where there is no capacity for choice, the problem of the right to freedom logically does not arise. If, as seems to be the case, the prohibition of cruelty can somehow be recast in terms of the negative right to welfare, what is left is the problem of the right to life. Apropos of this, it has been claimed that, in the instance of beings so simple as not to be able to have intentions and goals, consciousness is not a unified stream in any real sense.[34] Were it so, the existence of the beings in question would only be a succession of momentary states whose interruption could fail to be a harm for anyone, since there would be no individual "experiencer" whom the experiences could be said to belong to; and, obviously, in the case of such entities, it wouldn't be arbitrary not to take into consideration the right to life. This view has been vigorously challenged, however, and the matter remains controversial. Whatever the settlement of this problem, at any rate, it is important to stress here that, since what we developed is an *ad hominem* argument, the defense of the overall plausibility of the comparative criterion finally lies with the advocates of human rights doctrine.

Having thus reached the end of our argument, we can endeavor to advance an answer to the question we started from—to the question, that is, of whether human rights theory can be considered as a plausible preliminary solution also for the problems of a community broader than the human one.

The answer is affirmative. For it is clear that, on the basis of the very doctrine that establishes them, human rights are not *human*. On the one hand, the more or less avowed acceptance of the idea that species membership is not morally relevant has de facto eliminated from the best foundation of the theory any structural reference to the possession of a genotype *Homo sapiens*. And, on the other, the will to secure equal fundamental rights to all human beings, including the non-paradigmatic ones, has implied that the characteristics appealed to in order to justify the ascription of such rights could no longer be those (seen as) typically human but should instead lie at a cognitive-emotive level accessible to a large number of nonhuman animals. In this sense, not only is there nothing in the doctrine of human rights to motivate the reference to our species present in the phrase but it is the same justificatory argument underlying it that drives us toward the attribution of human rights to members of species other than our own.

Which, exactly, among nonhuman animals meet the requisites for inclusion in the privileged area of full moral status is a problem that cannot yet be settled in detail. However, among the beings that an *expanded theory of human rights* should cover there undoubtedly are mammals and birds, and probably vertebrates in general. I do not deem it necessary to restate here the cumulative case for this claim, which is supported by common sense as well.[35] Rather, it is worth stressing that, in defining grey areas or borderline cases, it is important to keep oneself open to the complexity of reality, avoiding recourse to what in the scientific domain has been called "the discontinuous mind."[36]

What, then, is the relationship between the expanded theory of human rights and the accounts of welfare and of the value of life examined above? Which solutions does it advance for the problems we left unresolved? From now on, we will set aside the moral community as a whole and will focus instead on the characteristics of the more limited area that includes the holders of full moral status.

The first thing to notice is that, in fact, the theory does not offer an answer to all the questions. What has been identified as the minimal basis for organized cohabitation—the doctrine that embraces the fundamental moral values to be realized in any acceptable society—

gives center stage only to the question of the basic treatment of hold-ers of full moral status. In other words, the dilemmas created by the search for criteria to resolve possible conflicts between right-holders are not confronted. And yet, contrary to what might appear, this does not represent a limitation.

The reason for this lies in the already mentioned peculiarities of the expanded theory. In the first place, since it is a doctrine centered on noninterference, it does not involve distributive problems that might imply the necessity of attributing differential value to the beings involved. Second, as the resort to the language of rights makes clear, the perspective within which the theory roots is deontological rather than consequentialist. Given that rights are side constraints on pos-sible forms of utilitarian aggregation, it is evident that any form of maximizing sacrifice is excluded a priori. Since, therefore, nobody can be permissibly sacrificed for the benefit of others, the problem of a possible attribution of differential value does not arise in this respect either. Finally, the fact that the doctrine refers to the institutional level—that it deals, that is, with codified or official violations—implies that the problem of possible interindividual conflicts is set aside in order to focus only on the relationship between social power and the individuals who make up the collectivity.

Within the limits of the area it actually covers, on the other hand—that is, where it is only a matter of determining the seriousness of possible institutional violations of the negative rights involved—the expanded theory, as we have seen, excludes perfectionism not only in the case of the interests in welfare and freedom but also when it comes to the interest in continued existence.[37] This means among other things that, as far as the value of life is concerned, it rejects both the view that attributes a direct role to self-consciousness and the quali-tative approach that grants special weight to characteristics other than the inclusive one; and that, among subjective-quantitative accounts, it dismisses both the external and the internal-proportional approaches. In other words, what we are confronting is just that egalitarian the-sis not only about welfare but also about lives that many regard as utterly counterintuitive and that we described as paralyzing.

Is this a paradoxical result? No, if once again one takes into account the fact that human rights come into being as institutional restric-tions. In view of such a framework, in fact, it is plausible to claim that the egalitarian thesis turns out to be the most intuitive. For none of us holds that slavery could be prohibited in the case of individuals with a high IQ but be permissible in the case of individuals with a lower IQ; or that a massacre of intellectuals is a more serious violation of human rights than a massacre of intellectually disabled children. When it comes to official violations of basic rights, we deem any hierarchical scale morally repugnant. It is partly in this light that, I believe, one should look at the differences between the egalitarianism of the expanded theory of rights and the perfectionist inclinations of the quality-of-life doctrine such as it is taking shape and becoming prominent in the bioethical field.

This point is worth developing. Bioethics endeavors to issue precepts for two practical spheres: that of the individual treatment of the patient and that of the definition of general criteria, often legal or institutional in character. The former sphere obviously cannot conflict with the expanded theory of rights, for it does not relate to official policies. The latter—that of institutional criteria—divides in turn, roughly speaking, into two branches. Of these, one, having to do with the policies of allocation of medical resources, concerns again an area that the expanded theory does not cover, as referring to welfare rights or positive rights—in particular the right to assistance. The other, however, directly affects the sphere of concern of the theory of rights, insofar as it relates to an attribution of differential status to specific classes of individuals aiming at being legally ratified.

To decide whether certain beings (for example, some or all nonhumans) can be experimented upon without side constraints, or whether certain beings (for example, newborn babies with severe physical and mental disabilities) can be deprived of the right to life means intervening on institutional questions of moral and legal status. When they propound, or sanction, such (re)structuring of official policies, therefore, the accounts based on the quality-of-life doctrine can come into conflict with the egalitarianism that underlies the (expanded) theory of human rights. As the heated controversy on nonvoluntary euthanasia shows, as far as human beings are concerned, the existence of a contradiction has already been clearly grasped by some.[38] In the case of nonhumans, on the other hand, the problem arises at a higher level: the presently suggested classifications based on quality-of-life criteria have in fact the effect of blurring the force of the case for the extension of human rights to members of other species endowed with intentionality.

The Fundamental Step

In a recent volume, the American legal scholar Gary Francione claimed that the characterization of nonhumans—from now on, I shall use this term to refer only to nonhumans endowed with intentionality—as property is the main impediment placed in the way of any attempt to extend basic rights beyond the boundaries of the species *Homo sapiens*.[39] In the light of this, he has argued that the first right to be afforded in such a context is the right not to be treated as mere means to others' ends.

The application of the line of reasoning so far developed to the current situation of our societies leads to a like conclusion. With an important difference, however: that the removal of nonhumans from the category of things or items of property is not seen as the implementation of a particular right but rather as the essential condition for a translation at the social level of the implications of the expanded theory. Within the framework of the feminist debate on equality, it has been emphasized that in case of serious disparity in access to rights, the fundamental step to be made regards what could be defined as juridical equality as a legal principle in itself.[40] If, so far as women are concerned, this takes the form of a law on equality that may play an active role in fostering social transformation, in the case of nonhumans what is in question is instead a legal change aimed at removing in the status of property the basic obstacle to the enjoyment of the denied rights. In this sense, the shift from the condition of objects to that of subjects of legal rights does not appear as a point of arrival but rather as the initial access to the circle of possible beneficiaries of that "egalitarian plateau" from which contemporary political philosophy starts in order to determine any more specific individual right.[41]

In order to better understand this point, consider the current situation. Billions of nonhuman animals are tortured, confined, and killed for our benefit. In a real sense, the actual parallel for the condition of these beings is slavery, that is, the practice by which human beings are reduced to assets in the strict meaning of that term ("live articles of property" was the telling Aristotelian definition of slaves.)[42] In nineteenth century United States, for example, slaves were institutionally dispossessed of their own goals, and their welfare, their freedom, and their lives were under the control of others. Only with the abolition of slavery through the Thirteenth Amendment to the Constitution was the fundamental inequality precluding access to nearly any other moral and legal protections removed. A reorganization of society along the lines of the expanded theory likewise requires the constitutional abolition of the status of mere assets of nonhuman animals, and the prohibition of all the practices that are today made possible by such status, from raising for food to scientific experimentation to the most varied forms of commercial use and systematic extermination.[43]

These are the conclusions to which we are led by an argument that is neither contingent nor eccentric but is the necessary dialectical derivation of the most universally accepted among contemporary ethical doctrines—human rights theory. In this sense, the normative force of the demands of the expanded theory entails a commitment not only to avoid participating in, but also to oppose, present discrimination.[44] And this because the institutional denial of fundamental rights to beings that are entitled to them does not simply deprive the victims of the objects of their rights, but is a direct attack on those very rights themselves. In other words, such a denial subverts not merely what is right, but the very idea of justice.

Notes

Chapter 1

1. Cf. Steve F. Sapontzis, "Everyday Morality and Animal Rights," Between the Species, vol. 3 (1987), sect. 3.

2. Richard Wasserstrom, "Rights, Human Rights, and Racial Discrimination," in *Moral Problems*, ed. James Rachels, 3d ed. (New York: Harper & Row, 1979), p. 7. The article originally appeared in *Journal of Philosophy*, vol. 61 (1964).

3. On the subject see David Brion Davis, *The Problem of Slavery in Western Culture* (Ithaca: Cornell University Press, 1969), chap. 13.

4. This holds true for authors as different in normative propensities as John Rawls and Richard M. Hare. In this connection see Hare's own remarks in "Rules of War and Moral Reasoning," *Philosophy & Public Affairs*, vol. 1 (1972).

5. Mary Warnock, *Ethics since 1900*, 3d ed. (Oxford: Oxford University Press, 1978), p. 132.

6. Sanford H. Kadish, "Respect for Life and Regard for Rights in the Criminal Law," in *Respect for Life in Medicine, Philosophy, and the Law*, ed. Stephen F. Barker (Baltimore: John Hopkins University Press, 1977), cited in Helga Kuhse, *The Sanctity-of-Life Doctrine in Medicine. A Critique* (Oxford: Clarendon Press, 1987), p. 10.

7. Nearly all authors add "innocent."

8. I say "almost" since many advocates of the doctrine, while maintaining that it is absolutely forbidden intentionally to kill or to let die a patient, accept the idea that it is sometimes permissible "to abstain from preventing death." For a discussion of this, see among others Helga Kuhse, *The Sanctity-of-Life Doctrine in Medicine*, pp. 23 ff.

9. For the details of Tony Bland's story see Peter Singer, *Rethinking Life and Death. The Collapse of Our Traditional Ethics* (Oxford: Oxford University Press, 1995), chap. 4.

10. Joseph Fletcher, *Humanhood: Essays in Biomedical Ethics* (New York: Prometheus Books, 1980), pp. 12–16.

11. James Rachels, *The End of Life. Euthanasia and Morality* (Oxford: Oxford University Press 1986), pp. 24–27.

12. Cf. P. Singer, *Rethinking Life and Death,* p. 67.

13. On the aspect of interindividual conflict, see Judith Jarvis Thompson, "A Defense of Abortion," *Philosophy & Public Affairs,* vol. 1 (1971). See also Harlan B. Miller, "On Abortion" (1993), part 5. (http://server.phil.vt.edu/miller/papers/abortion.html).

14. Cf. Donna Haraway, *Primate Visions. Gender, Race, and Nature in the World of Modern Science* (New York: Routledge, 1989), pp. 197–203.

15. Cf. Colin McGinn, "Animal Minds, Animal Morality," *Social Research,* vol. 62 (1995): 740–741.

16. M. Marx and W. Hillix, *Systems and Theories in Psychology* (New York: McGraw-Hill, 1967), p. 168, cited in Bernard E. Rollin, *The Unheeded Cry. Animal Consciousness, Animal Pain and Science* (Oxford: Oxford University Press, 1990), p. 75. Rollins's volume provides a comprehensive discussion of the entire question, from which I benefited.

17. See for example Maxine Sheets-Johnstone, "Taking Evolution Seriously: A Matter of Primate Intelligence," *Etica & Animali,* vol. 8 (1996): 119–120. Sheets-Johnstone also puts forth an interesting objection to the behavioristic use of the canon. If it is true, as it has been claimed, that what Morgan—himself a staunch upholder of animal consciousness—was enunciating was, rather than a principle of simplicity, a general evolutionary principle, then far from defending a cleavage between humans and nonhumans, his idea would simply be anchored in the fact that lower forms of intelligence developed before higher ones and are thus represented to a greater degree in the evolutionary world.

18. Marc Bekoff, "Cognitive Ethology: The Comparative Study of Animal Minds," in *Blackwell Companion to Cognitive Science,* ed. W. Bechtel and G. Graham (Oxford: Blackwell, 1998), pp. 371–379. Cf. also Marc Bekoff and Colin Allen, "Cognitive Ethology: Slayers, Skeptics, and Proponents," in *Anthropomorphism, Anecdotes, and Animals,* ed. Robert W. Mitchell, Nicholas S. Thompson, and H. Lyn White Miles (Albany: State University of New York Press, 1997).

19. Cf. James Rachels, *Created from Animals. The Moral Implications of Darwinism* (Oxford: Oxford University Press, 1990), p. 142. I slightly modified the example.

20. Thomas Nagel, "What Is It Like to Be a Bat?" *Philosophical Review,* vol. 83 (1974).

21. John R. Searle, "Animal Minds," *Etica & Animali,* vol. 9 (1998): 49–50.

22. The statement is from Donald R. Griffin, *Animal Minds* (Chicago: The University of Chicago Press, 1992), p. 57. For the introduction of the phrase "cognitive ethology" see Donald R. Griffin, *The Question of Animal Awareness* (New York: The Rockefeller University Press, 1976), chap. 7. Cf. also Donald R. Griffin, *Animal Thinking* (Cambridge, Mass.: Harvard University Press, 1984). For an outline of the history of, and of recent developments in, cognitive ethology, cf. Colin Allen and Marc Bekoff, *Species of Mind: The Philosophy and Biology of Cognitive Ethology* (Cambridge, Mass.: MIT Press, 1997).

23. For a summary see Jane Goodall, *The Chimpanzees of Gombe* (Cambridge: Cambridge University Press, 1989).

24. The thesis is put forward in Barbara Noske, "Great Apes as Anthropological Subjects—Deconstructing Anthropocentrism," in *The Great Ape Project. Equality beyond Humanity,* ed. Paola Cavalieri and Peter Singer (New York: St. Martin's Press, 1994). On recent changes in ethology and primatology see also Volker Sommer, " 'Sind Affen denn auch Leute?' Ja. Denn zwischen Natur und Kultur fließen die Übergänge," *Etica & Animali,* vol. 8 (1996).

25. For a particularly illustrative example of the new approach see Joyce H. Poole, "An Exploration of a Commonality between Ourselves and Elephants," *Etica & Animali,* vol. 9 (1998).

26. Charles Darwin, "The Descent of Man," in C. Darwin, *The Origin of Species and The Descent of Man* (New York: Random House, n.d.), pp. 461–465.

27. See sect. 2 in Paola Cavalieri and Peter Singer, eds., *The Great Ape Project.*

28. Cf. Louis M. Herman, Adam A. Pack, and Palmer Morrel-Samuels, "Representational and Conceptual Skills of Dolphins," in *Language and Communication: Comparative Perspectives,* ed. H. L. Roitblat, Louis M. Herman, and P. E. Nachtigall (Hillsdale, N.J.: Lawrence Erlbaum Associates, 1993), and Louis M. Herman, Adam A. Pack, and Amy M. Wood, "Bottlenose Dolphins Can Generalize Rules and Develop Abstract Concepts," *Marine Mammal Science,* vol. 10 (1994). See also, more generally, Denise L. Herzing and Thomas I. White, "Dolphins and the Question of Personhood," *Etica & Animali,* vol. 9 (1998).

29. See the interview with Irene Pepperberg in Eugene Linden, "Can Animals Think?" *Time,* 29 Mar. 1993. Cf. also I. Pepperberg, "A Communicative Approach to Animal Cognition: A Study of Conceptual Abilities of an African Grey Parrot," in *Cognitive Ethology: The Minds of Other Animals,* ed. Carolyn A. Ristau (Hillsdale, N.J.: Lawrence Erlbaum Associates, 1991).

30. On these three elements, and in particular on Grice's approach, cf. Robert W. Mitchell, "Humans, Nonhumans and Personhood," in *The Great Ape Project,* ed. Paola Cavalieri and Peter Singer. A useful synthesis of the theoretical problems with specific reference to primatological studies can be found in Andrew Whiten, "Imitation, Pretense and Mindreading: Secondary Representation in Comparative Primatology and Developmental Psychology?" in *Reaching into Thought. The Minds of the Great Apes,* ed. Ann E. Russon, Kim A. Bard, and Sue Taylor Parker (Cambridge: Cambridge University Press, 1996).

31. On Bateson's side can be found for example Marc Bekoff and Colin Allen: cf. among other things "Intentional Communication and Social Play: How and Why Animals Negotiate and Agree to Play," in *Animal Play: Evolutionary, Comparative, and Ecological Perspectives,* ed. Marc Bekoff and J. A. Byers (Cambridge: Cambridge University Press, 1998).

32. A good summary can be found in Donald R. Griffin, *Animal Minds,* chap. 3.

33. Ibid., p. 155.

34. Juan Carlos Gómez, "Are Apes Persons? The Case for Primate Intersubjectivity," *Etica & Animali,* vol. 9 (1998): 58–60.

35. David Morgan, "Scientists: Apes Have Strong Communication Skills," Reuters, *News America Digital Publishing,* 15 Feb. 1998.

Chapter 2

1. Alasdair C. MacIntyre, *After Virtue. A Study in Moral Theory* (Notre Dame: University of Notre Dame Press, 1984). For the quotation, see p. 10.

2. Ibid., chap. 3.

3. An interesting discussion of this aspect can be found in Carlo Foppa, "L'insoutenable poids de la théorie de l'évolution," *Etica & Animali,* vol. 8 (1996).

4. Mary Warnock, *Ethics since 1900,* 3d ed. (Oxford: Oxford University Press, 1990), p. 105.

5. See Henry Sidgwick, *The Methods of Ethics,* 7th ed. (1907) (Indianapolis: Hackett Publishing Company, 1981), in particular book 1, chap. 3 and book 4, concluding chapter. On the subject of Sidgwick's position on the autonomy of ethics, see J. B. Schneewind, *Sidgwick's Ethics and Victorian Moral Philosophy* (Oxford: Clarendon Press, 1977), pp. 204 ff.

6. James Rachels, *Created from Animals. The Moral Implications of Darwinism* (Oxford: Oxford University Press, 1990), p. 114.

7. Still referred in W. K. Frankena, "The Concept of Morality," *Journal of Philosophy,* vol. 63 (1966), and in G. J. Warnock, *The Object of Morality* (London: Methuen, 1971), in particular chap. 2 and chap. 5, to all forms of conduct involving beings other than the agent, and thus to beneficence as

well, the notion of morality in the narrow sense tends later on to focus on nonmaleficence in authors like J. L. Mackie, *Ethics. Inventing Right and Wrong* (London: Penguin, 1990), pp. 107–108, and Josef Raz, "Right-based Moralities," in *Theories of Rights,* ed. Jeremy Waldron, (Oxford: Oxford University Press, 1984), p. 197.

8. John Stuart Mill, "Utilitarianism," in J. S. Mill, *On Liberty and Other Essays* (Oxford: Oxford University Press, 1998), pp. 195–196.

9. Thomas Nagel, "Ethics as an Autonomous Theoretical Subject," in *Morality as a Biological Phenomenon,* ed. Gunther S. Stent (Berkeley: University of California Press, 1978).

10. Cf. Harlan B. Miller, "Science, Ethics, and Moral Status," *Between the Species,* vol. 10 (1994): 14.

11. Ibid. See also Steve F. Sapontzis, *Morals, Reason, and Animals* (Philadelphia: Temple University Press, 1987), pp. 146 ff.

12. Ibid., pp. 41 ff.

13. G. J. Warnock, *The Object of Morality,* p. 148.

14. Mark Twain, *Huckleberry Finn,* quoted in Edward Johnson, *Species and Morality,* Ph.D. diss., Princeton University, July 1976 (University Microfilms International, Ann Arbor, Mich.) p. 21.

15. Robert Nozick, *Anarchy, State and Utopia* (New York: Basic Books, 1974), p. 39.

16. L. Wayne Sumner, *Abortion and Moral Theory* (Princeton, N.J.: Princeton University Press, 1981), chap. 1, sect. 5.

17. Ibid., p. 32.

18. James Rachels, *Created from Animals,* pp. 176 ff.

19. In *Moral Status* (Oxford: Clarendon Press, 1997, p. 55), Mary Anne Warren remarks that in theory there can be consciousness without there being sentience; however, she agrees that in the world as we know it, the two aspects are always present together. It is worth stressing that the form of consciousness we are here referring to is construed in the traditional sense and not in the weakened sense (inwardness) that is mentioned by Hans Jonas in *The Phenomenon of Life* (Chicago: University of Chicago Press, 1966, p. 58). On Jonas and the beginning of "inwardness" see Carlo Foppa, "L'ontologie de Hans Jonas à la lumière de la théorie de l'évolution," in *Nature et descendance. Hans Jonas et le principe "Responsailité,"* ed. Denis Müller and René Simon (Lausanne: Labor et Fides, 1993).

20. J. Baird Callicott, "Animal Liberation: A Triangular Affair," *Environmental Ethics,* vol. 2 (1980).

21. Actually, the situation is more complicated since, as we will see later on, one or more of the characteristics belonging to the first area can be construed in objectivistic terms. We can however lay aside this complication for the moment. On the characteristics of objective theories, see David DeGrazia, *Taking Animals Seriously: Mental Life and Moral Status* (Cambridge: Cambridge University Press, 1996), pp. 216 ff.

22. Thomas Nagel, *The Possibility of Altruism* (Oxford: Clarendon Press, 1970), p. 145.

23. Aldo Leopold, *A Sand County Almanac* (New York: Oxford University Press, 1949), p. 129.

24. Peter Singer, *Practical Ethics* (Cambridge: Cambridge University Press, 1979), p. 92.

25. On the subject of the normativity of the self, see Paola Cavalieri and Harlan B. Miller, "Automata, Receptacles and Selves," *Psyche. An interdisciplinary journal of research on consciousness,* vol. 5 (1999) (http://psyche.cs.monash.edu.au/v5/psyche-5–04-cavalieri.html).

26. For Albert Schweitzer, see *Civilization and Ethics,* 3d ed. (London: A. C. Black, 1949), p. 344. A more recent version of the ethics of reverence for life can be found in Paul Taylor, *Respect for Nature* (Princeton: Princeton University Press, 1986). For William K. Frankena, see "Ethics and the Environment," in *Ethics and Problems of the 21st Century,* ed. Kenneth E. Goodpaster and Kenneth M. Sayre (Notre Dame: University of Notre Dame Press, 1979), p. 11.

27. See also DeGrazia, *Taking Animals Seriously,* pp. 250–254.

28. For an example of an atomistic approach see Kenneth Goodpaster, "From Egoism to Environmentalism," in *Ethics and Problems of the 21st Century,* ed. Kenneth E. Goodpaster and Kenneth M. Sayre.

29. H. Sidgwick, *The Methods of Ethics,* p. 79.

30. David Hume, *A Treatise of Human Nature* (Oxford: Oxford University Press, 1888), p. 469.

31. In "Hume's *Is/Ought* Dichotomy and the Relation of Ecology to Leopold's Land Ethic," *Environmental Ethics,* vol. 4 (1982), J. Baird Callicott appeals to an interpretation by MacIntyre to develop an argument that he holds can overcome the difficulty raised by Hume's Law. According to MacIntyre in his "Hume on 'Is' and 'Ought,' " in *The Is/Ought Question,* ed. W. D. Hudson (London: Macmillan, 1969), Hume, rather than absolutely denying the possibility of getting from *is* to *ought,* merely criticizes the ways in which this transition is traditionally made, matching them with a different route, which appeals to bridge notions able to fill the logical gap between the descriptive and the normative, and assembled under the heading of the passions. Compendiously, Callicott's argument is the following: psychologically, we are endowed with positive sentiments—"passions"—for the community in which we live; these sentiments have normative value; ecology and the environmental sciences show us that our community does not consist only of the society we live in, but also of the natural environment within which we exist (Leopold's "land"); our positive sentiments should therefore be extended to include the environment. But here Callicott misinterprets MacIntyre. Whether or not it may be ascribable to Hume, the view that MacIntyre advances does not consider as bridge notions between *is* and *ought* the passions in the sense of *morally favorable attitudes* but rather the pas-

sions in the more basic sense of *desires, needs, and the like.* Such an idea seems plausible—and somehow parallels the idea defended here that subjectivity, as a seat of positive and negative experiences, is the only direct source of normativity. Just because of this reason, however, it cannot be appealed to by those who want to defend the inclusion of nonconscious entities in the moral community.

32. J. Baird Callicott, "Intrinsic Value in Nature: A Metaethical Analysis," *Electronic Journal of Analytic Philosophy,* vol. 3 (1995), paragraphs 4 and 5 (http://www.phil.indiana.edu/ejap/1995.spring/callicott.abs.html).

33. For a brilliant defense of this view see Colin McGinn, "Animal Minds, Animal Morality," *Social Research,* vol. 62 (1995).

34. David Gauthier, "Intervista," ed. Lorenzo Sacconi, *Notizie di Politeia,* vol. 4 (1988). For Gauthier's general approach see *Morals by Agreement* (Oxford: Clarendon Press, 1986).

35. I borrow the expression "silver rule" from Edward Johnson, *Species and Morality,* p. 134.

36. Colin McGinn, "Animal Minds, Animal Morality," p. 735.

Chapter 3

1. The phrase is borrowed from Peter Singer. See *Animal Liberation,* 2d ed. (New York: The New York Review of Books, 1990), p. 200.

2. René Descartes, "Discourse on the Method," in R. Descartes, *Discourse on the Method and Meditations on First Philosophy,* ed. David Weissman (New Haven & London: Yale University Press, 1996), part 3, p. 16.

3. Ibid., part 4, pp. 21–22.

4. Ibid., part 5, pp. 33–34.

5. Ibid., part 1, p. 4.

6. Letter to the Marquess of Newcastle, 23 Nov. 1646, included in *Descartes: Philosophical Letters,* trans. Anthony Kenny (1970) and partially reprinted in Tom Regan and Peter Singer, eds., *Animal Rights and Human Obligations* (Englewood Cliffs, N.J.: Prentice-Hall, 1976), p. 64.

7. Letter to Henry Moore, 5 Feb. 1649, included in *Descartes: Philosophical Letters,* trans. Anthony Kenny (1970), and partially reprinted in Tom Regan and Peter Singer, eds., *Animal Rights and Human Obligations,* p. 66.

8. René Descartes, "Discourse on the Method," in R. Descartes, *Discourse on the Method and Meditations on First Philosophy,* part 5, p. 36.

9. Aristotle, *Nicomachean Ethics,* X, 5, 1176a.

10. The phrase *"oi alloi empsychoi"* is Porphyry's and can be found in *De abstinentia.* Note, as it were, the strong anti-Cartesian tone of the term *empsychoi.*

11. In the letter to the Marquess of Newcastle cited above, he states in fact: "I cannot share the opinion of Montaigne and others who attribute understanding or thought to animals." And further on: "Montaigne and Charron

may have said that there is more difference between one human being and another than between a human being and an animal. . . ." See Tom Regan and Peter Singer, eds., *Animal Rights and Human Obligations,* pp. 63–64.

12. Peter Carruthers, "Brute Experience," *Journal of Philosophy,* vol. 86 (1989): 258–269.

13. Peter Carruthers, "Natural Theories of Consciousness," *European Journal of Philosophy,* vol. 2 (1998)

14. For a discussion of this point see P. Cavalieri and H. B. Miller, "Automata, Receptacles and Selves," *Psyche. An interdisciplinary journal of research on consciousness,* vol. 5 (1999) (http://psyche.cs.monash.edu.au/v5/psyche-5–04-cavalieri.html).

15. Raymond Frey, *Interests and Rights* (Oxford: Clarendon Press, 1980), p. 89. Frey subsequently dropped this view.

16. John R. Searle, "Animal Minds," *Etica & Animali,* vol. 9 (1998): 44.

17. Ibid., p. 43. The example is taken from Donald Davidson.

18. Ibid., pp. 37–38.

19. Immanuel Kant, *Lectures on Ethics,* trans. Louis Infield (New York: Harper and Row, 1963), p. 239.

20. Aristotle, *Politics,* I, 3, 1256 b.

21. Thomas Aquinas, *Summa contra Gentiles,* book 3, part 2, chap. 112.

22. Joseph Rickaby, "Ethics and Natural Law," in *Moral Philosophy* (1901), partially reprinted in Tom Regan and Peter Singer, eds., *Animal Rights and Human Obligations,* p. 180.

23. Thomas Aquinas, *Summa contra Gentiles,* book 3, part 2, chap. 112.

24. Ursula Wolf, *Das Tier in der Moral* (Frankfurt:Vittorio Klostermann, 1990), pp. 37–38.

25. Immanuel Kant, *Lectures on Ethics,* p. 239.

26. Ibid., p. 240.

27. Elisabeth M. Pybus and Alexander Broadie, "Kant on the Maltreatment of Animals," *Philosophy,* vol. 53 (1978): 560–561.

28. The course was apparently given at an indeterminate time between 1775 and 1780, hence at least five years before the publication of *Foundations of the Metaphysics of Morals.*

29. Immanuel Kant, *Foundations of the Metaphysics of Morals,* trans. Lewis W. Beck (Upper Saddle River, N.J.: Prentice-Hall, 1997), p. 38.

30. Ibid., p. 45.

31. Ibid., p. 46. In defining "second" this formulation, I keep to the most common judgment, which does not see the formulation referring to the "universal law of nature" as an independent version of the imperative (ibid., p. 38).

32. Kenneth E. Goodpaster, "From Egoism to Environmentalism" in *Ethics and Problems of the 21st Century*, ed. Kenneth E. Goodpaster and Kenneth M. Sayre (Notre Dame: University of Notre Dame Press, 1979), p. 34, n. 14.

33. David Ross, *Kant's Ethical Theory* (Oxford: Clarendon Press, 1954), quoted in Christina Hoff, *The Moral Domain: An Inquiry into Its Extent and*

Limits, Ph.D. diss., Brandeis University, May 1979 (University Microfilms International, Ann Arbor, Mich.), p. 58.

34. Christina Hoff, ibid., pp. 56–57.

35. Immanuel Kant, *Lectures on Ethics,* pp. 148–154.

36. Immanuel Kant, *Foundations of the Metaphysics of Morals,* p. 45.

37. Ibid.

38. Ibid., p. 51.

39. Working within the utilitarian tradition (although tinged with Kantianism), Richard Hare always bore in Mind, and often cited, the case of non-humans—see, for example, *Freedom and Reason* (Oxford: Clarendon Press, 1990), pp. 222 ff. Moreover, though he did not devote specific studies to the topic, he had occasion to stress that his views on the status of members of other species are the same as Peter Singer's (personal communication).

40. Immanuel Kant, *Foundations of the Metaphysics of Morals,* p. 40.

41. Onora O'Neill, "Kantian Ethics," in *A Companion to Ethics,* ed. Peter Singer (Oxford: Blackwell, 1991), p. 178.

42. Ibid., p. 184.

43. Immanuel Kant, *Foundations of the Metaphysics of Morals,* p. 51.

44. Arthur Schopenhauer, *On the Basis of Morality,* trans. E. F. J. Payne (Indianapolis: Bobbs-Merrill, 1965), p. 91.

45. Edward Johnson, *Species and Morality,* p. 195.

46. Leonard Nelson, "Duties to Animals," lecture given before 1927 and published posthumously in Germany in 1932, included in *A System of Ethics,* trans. N. Guterman (1956), and reprinted in Stanley and Roslind Godlovitch and John Harris, eds., *Animals, Men and Morals* (New York: Grove Press, 1972), p. 152. (Italics added).

47. Jeremy Bentham, *An Introduction to the Principles of Morals and Legislation* (New York: Hafner Press, 1948), chap. 1, 1.

48. On this point, see in particular David Fate Norton, "Hume, Atheism, and the Autonomy of Morals," in *Hume's Philosophy of Religion,* ed. M. Hester (Winston Salem: Wake Forest University Press, 1986).

49. *An Introduction to the Principles of Morals and Legislation,* chap. 17, 4, note 1.

50. *Animal Liberation,* pp. 7–8.

51. Jeremy Bentham, *An Introduction to The Principles of Morals and Legislation,* chap. 1, 11.

52. Ibid., chap. 17, 7.

53. Ibid., chap. 3, 2–4.

54. John Stuart Mill, "Dr. Whewell on Moral Philosophy" (1867), partially reprinted in Tom Regan and Peter Singer, eds. *Animal Rights and Human Obligations,* pp. 131–132.

55. Henry Sidgwick, *The Methods of Ethics,* 7th ed. (1907) (Indianapolis: Hackett Publishing Company, 1981), p. 414.

56. Edward Johnson, "Treating the Dirt: Environmental Ethics and Moral

Theory," in *Earthbound,* ed. Tom Regan (Philadelphia: Temple University Press, 1984), p. 340.

57. Jeremy Bentham, *An Introduction to the Principles of Morals and Legislation,* chap. 17, 4, note 1.

58. The criticism is reluctantly raised by Peter Singer himself in *Animal Liberation,* p. 210.

59. Henry Sidgwick, *The Methods of Ethics,* p. 241.

60. John Stuart Mill, "Utilitarianism," in J. S. Mill, *On Liberty and Other Essays* (Oxford: Oxford University Press, 1998), p. 140.

61. Ibid., p. 139.

62. Cf. David DeGrazia, *Taking Animals Seriously. Mental Life and Moral Status* (Cambridge: Cambridge University Press, 1996), pp. 240–241.

63. See in particular G. E. Moore, *Principia Ethica* (Cambridge: Cambridge University Press, 1993). Curiously enough, the utilitarian legacy was somehow taken up by a philosopher who expressed himself in the language of rights, Henry S. Salt. Salt's position, as expressed in his *Animals' Rights* (London, 1892; new edition, London: Centaur Press, 1980), remained however utterly marginal with respect to mainstream English philosophy.

Chapter 4

1. Alan Gewirth, *Reason and Morality* (Chicago: University of Chicago Press, 1978), p. 317.

2. Richard Rorty, "Human Rights, Rationality and Sentimentality," in *On Human Rights,* ed. Stephen Shute and Susan Hurley (New York: Basic Books, 1993), p. 125. The remark is made in the context of a case for the moral relevance of the species boundary even in the absence of any morally significant human "essence."

3. Ibid.

4. Peter Singer, *Animal Liberation,* 2d ed. (New York: The New York Review of Books, 1990), p. 9.

5. Michael Tooley, *Abortion and Infanticide* (Oxford: Oxford University Press, 1983), p. 10. More precisely, Tooley asserts that there are two basic lines of criticism: on one side, ethical positions can be criticized on purely logical grounds; on the other, it is possible to show the implausibility of some of the nonethical claims upon which these positions often rest.

6. David Richards, *A Theory of Reasons for Action* (Oxford: Clarendon Press, 1971), p. 83.

7. On the circularity of Richards's argument see Paola Cavalieri and Will Kymlicka, "Expanding the Social Contract," *Etica & Animali,* vol.8 (1996): 30–31, note 8.

8. Bernard Williams, "The Idea of Equality," in *Moral Concepts,* ed. Joel Feinberg (Oxford: Oxford University Press, 1970), p. 156.

9. Lectures for the seminar "Contrattualismo ed etica," held in Naples from

21 Feb. to 24 Mar. 1994 at the "Istituto Universitario Suor Orsola Benincasa." The material of these unpublished lectures has been used in a revised form in Thomas Scanlon, *What We Owe to Each Other* (Cambridge, Mass.: Harvard University Press, 1998), where the appeal to what is typical of one's kind is proposed again (pp.185–186).

10. Michael Tooley, *Abortion and Infanticide,* p. 71. On this point see also Michael Tooley, "Speciesism and Basic Moral Principles," *Etica & Animali,* vol. 9 (1998), sect. 5.

11. James Rachels, *Created from Animals. The Moral Implications of Darwinism* (Oxford: Oxford University Press, 1990), pp. 173–174, 194–197.

12. John Rawls, *A Theory of Justice* (Oxford: Oxford University Press, 1973), p. 126.

13. Robert Nozick, *Anarchy, State and Utopia* (New York: Basic Books, 1974), p. 49.

14. An up-to-date, interesting survey can be found in Daniel A. Dombrowski, *Babies and Beasts. The Argument from Marginal Cases* (Chicago: University of Illinois Press, 1997).

15. Carl Cohen, "The Case for the Use of Animals in Biomedical Research," *New England Journal of Medicine* 315 (1986): 866.

16. Linnaeus's letter to J. G. Gmelin, 1747, published in Edward L. Green, "Linnaeus as an Evolutionist," *Proc. Washington Acad. of Sc.,* vol. 11 (1909): 25–26, cited in Carl Sagan and Ann Druyan, *Shadows of Forgotten Ancestors* (New York: Random House, 1992), p. 274.

17. See Jared Diamond, "The Third Chimpanzee," in *The Great Ape Project: Equality beyond Humanity,* ed. Paola Cavalieri and Peter Singer (New York: St. Martin's Press, 1994), p. 97. See also the statements made by the Australian geneticist Simon Easteal: Julian Cribb, "Now it's Homo Gorillas," *The Australian,* 3 May 1996, pp. 1 and 4.

18. See David DeGrazia's discussion in *Taking Animals Seriously. Mental Life and Moral Status* (Cambridge: Cambridge University Press, 1996), chap. 7. For a detailed, specific example focusing on the gradational nature of self-consciousness, see Maxine Sheets-Johnstone's analysis in "Consciousness: A Natural History," *Journal of Consciousness Studies,* vol. 5 (1998).

19. Donald R. Griffin, *Animal Minds* (Chicago: The University of Chicago Press, 1992), p. 254.

20. Robert Nozick, "About Mammals and People," *The New York Times Book Review,* 27 Nov. 1983.

21. James Rachels, *Created from Animals,* pp. 183–184.

22. Mary Midgley, *Animals and Why They Matter* (Athens: The University of Georgia Press, 1983), p. 124. Midgley defends her version of naturalism in "The Absence of a Gap between Facts and Values," *Aristotelian Society Supplementary,* vol. 54 (1980).

23. Peter Carruthers, *The Animals Issue* (Cambridge: Cambridge University Press, 1992).

24. Ibid., p. 116.

25. On the slippery slope argument see, among others, R. G. Frey, "The Fear of a Slippery Slope," in Gerald Dworkin, R. G. Frey, and Sissela Bok, *Euthanasia and Physician-Assisted Suicide* (Cambridge: Cambridge University Press, 1998), pp. 43–47, where useful bibliographical suggestions can also be found.

26. John Rawls, *A Theory of Justice,* p. 506.

27. For a more exhaustive discussion see P. Cavalieri and W. Kymlicka, "Expanding the Social Contract," pp. 12–14.

28. Stanley Benn, "Egalitarianism and Equal Consideration of Interests," in *Nomos IX: Equality,* ed. J. Roland Pennock and John W. Chapman (New York: Atherton, 1967), p. 62.

29. See especially Michael Wreen, "In Defense of Speciesism," *Ethics & Animals,* vol. 5 (1984). This and other objections advanced by Wreen have been criticized in detail by Evelyn Pluhar. For a summary of the debate, cf. E. Pluhar, "Speciesism: A Form of Bigotry or a Justified View?" *Between the Species,* vol. 4 (1988).

30. See Edward Johnson's discussion in *Species and Morality,* Ph.D. diss., Princeton University, July 1976 (University Microfilms International, Ann Arbor, Mich.), pp. 150–154.

31. On this point see also Paola Cavalieri, "L'humanité au-delà des humains," *Le Débat* 108 (2000): 185–186.

Chapter 5

1. Peter Singer, *Animal Liberation,* 2d ed. (New York: The New York Review of Books, 1990), pp. 8–9. (Italics added.)

2. Ibid., p. 15.

3. Brian Barry, *Theories of Justice* (Berkeley: University of California Press, 1989), p. 204.

4. Peter Singer, *Animal Liberation,* p. 16.

5. Bernard Williams, "A Critique of Utilitarianism," in J. J. C. Smart and Bernard Williams, *Utilitarianism: For and Against* (Cambridge: Cambridge University Press, 1973), pp. 98 ff.

6. See, for example, Peter Singer, "Sidgwick and Reflective Equilibrium," *The Monist,* vol.58 (1974): 516.

7. "Utilitarianism", in J. S. Mill, *On Liberty and Other Essays* (Oxford: Oxford University Press, 1998), chap. 5, in particular pp. 189–190.

8. David Lyons, "Utility and Rights," in *Theories of Rights,* ed. Jeremy Waldron (Oxford: Oxford University Press, 1984), pp. 114, 132.

9. Tom Regan has devoted several essays to the subject of the moral status of nonhumans, some of which have been collected in the volume *All that Dwell Therein* (Berkeley: University of California Press, 1982). His main con-

tribution to the debate, however, is *The Case for Animal Rights* (Berkeley: University of California Press, 1983).

10. Joel Feinberg, *Social Philosophy* (Englewood Cliffs, N.J.: Prentice-Hall, 1973), chap. 4, and Joel Feinberg, *Rights, Justice and the Bounds of Liberty* (Princeton: Princeton University Press, 1980), chap. 2.

11. Tom Regan, *The Case for Animal Rights,* p. 243.

12. Arthur Schopenhauer, *On the Basis of Morality,* trans. E. F. J. Payne (Indianapolis: Bobbs-Merrill, 1965), p. 162.

13. Immanuel Kant, *The Philosophy of Law,* trans. W. Hastie (Edinburgh: T. & T. Clark, 1887), p. 195.

14. Tom Regan, *The Case for Animal Rights,* p. 262. (First italics added.)

15. Ibid., chap. 7, sect. 4, although, as Evelyn Pluhar remarks, the argument for equality suffers from internal inconsistency and circularity. See Evelyn Pluhar, *Beyond Prejudice. The Moral Significance of Human and Nonhuman Animals* (Durham: Duke University Press, 1995), p. 239.

16. Moreover, the exchange rate between the inner and the outer circle is not at par. With respect to beings that are not clearly subjects-of-a-life, however, Regan invites us to err on the side of caution, both "in view of our profound ignorance" and for the purpose of "fostering an environment in which individual rights are respected" (see Tom Regan, *The Case for Animal Rights,* pp. 319–320).

17. For a definition of the lifeboat situation see ibid., pp. 351–353, 385–387. Of course, cases of conflict also include self-defense and like circumstances, which are tackled in detail in chap. 8, sect. 7 but are not relevant here.

18. Ronald Dworkin, *Taking Rights Seriously* (Cambridge, Mass.: Harvard University Press, 1979), p. xi.

19. Tom Regan, *The Case for Animal Rights,* p. 243.

20. Recently, Regan has openly included birds among the beings that satisfy the subject-of-a life criterion and has translated such a criterion in terms of the interesting notion of "unified psychological presence." See Tom Regan, "Animal Rights," in *Encyclopedia of Animal Rights and Animal Welfare,* ed. Marc Bekoff with Carron A. Meaney (Westport, Conn.: Greenwood Press, 1998), pp. 42–43.

21. David DeGrazia, *Taking Animals Seriously. Mental Life and Moral Status* (Cambridge: Cambridge University Press, 1996). For the introduction of the notion of prima facie duties see W. D. Ross, *The Right and the Good* (Indianapolis: Hackett Publishing Company, 1988), p. 19.

22. For a concise presentation of the differences between foundationalism and coherentism, see Dale Jamieson, "Method and Moral Theory," in *A Companion to Ethics,* ed. Peter Singer (Oxford: Blackwell, 1991), pp. 480–484.

23. David DeGrazia, *Taking Animals Seriously,* pp. 44 ff.

24. Ibid., pp. 233–235.

25. Ibid., pp. 249, 254–257. See also a previous version of the thesis in David DeGrazia, "The Distinction between Equality in Moral Status and Deserving Equal Consideration," *Between the Species,* vol. 7 (1991).

26. David DeGrazia, *Taking Animals Seriously,* pp. 270–271.

27. Ibid., pp. 73, 266–268. It is obvious that the misery caused to other beings can come into play for many nonhumans as well, and that the effects on the fabric of the moral community, as I have already maintained while discussing the slippery slope argument, cannot be taken for granted.

28. Ibid., p. 70.

29. Ibid., p. 270.

30. See for example Peter Singer, *Practical Ethics* (Cambridge: Cambridge University Press, 1979), pp. 80–81. Actually, as we shall see in relation to quantitative theories, Singer's position is more complex. In this context, however, we can temporarily set aside this problem.

31. Donald VanDeVeer, "Whither Baby Doe?" in *Matters of Life and Death,* ed. Tom Regan, 2d ed. (New York: Random House, 1986), p. 238.

32. James Rachels, *Created from Animals. The Moral Implications of Darwinism* (Oxford: Oxford University Press, 1990), p. 198.

33. See Steve F. Sapontzis, *Morals, Reason, and Animals* (Philadelphia: Temple University Press, 1987), p. 161.

34. The choice theory is advanced by H. L. A. Hart, while the interest theory is defended by, among others, Joseph Raz.

35. See Michael Tooley, *Abortion and Infanticide* (Oxford: Oxford University Press, 1983). For an earlier version, see M. Tooley, "Abortion and Infanticide," *Philosophy & Public Affairs,* vol. 2 (1972).

36. See the criticisms advanced by James Rachels himself in "Do Animals Have a Right to Life?" in *Ethics and Animals,* ed. Harlan B. Miller and William H. Williams (Clifton N.J.: Humana Press, 1983), pp. 277–278. Tooley's conception of the subject of nonmomentary interests is avowedly influenced by Derek Parfit's views, which, after being previously stated in a few articles, are now in *Reasons and Persons* (Oxford: Oxford University Press, 1986), part 3.

37. Raymond G. Frey, "Animal Parts, Human Wholes," in *Biomedical Ethics Reviews,* ed. James M. Humber and Robert F. Almeder (Clifton, N.J.: Humana Press, 1987), p. 93.

38. Raymond G. Frey, "Autonomy and the Value of Animal Life," *The Monist,* vol. 70 (1987): 55.

39. On this point cf. Steve F. Sapontzis, "Autonomy as an Excuse for All-Too-Human Chauvinism," *Between the Species,* vol. 8 (1992).

40. David DeGrazia, *Taking Animals Seriously,* p. 250. Cf. the argument James Rachels advances with respect to the Kantian defense of the incomparable value of rational creatures in *Created from Animals,* pp. 201–202.

41. Peter Singer, *Rethinking Life and Death. The Collapse of Our Traditional Ethics* (Oxford: Oxford University Press, 1995), p. 191.

42. Peter Singer, *Practical Ethics,* pp. 89–90.

43. David DeGrazia, *Taking Animals Seriously,* p. 243. I am generally indebted to DeGrazia for this discussion. For an analysis of the difference between the basic form of imaginative identification and the imaginative process required by comparative evaluations such as those suggested by Mill and Singer, see Steve F. Sapontzis, "On Exploiting Inferiors," *Between the Species,* vol. 11 (1995): 7–11.

44. Peter Singer, *Practical Ethics,* p. 90.

45. Raymond G. Frey, "Animal Parts, Human Wholes," pp. 98 ff.

46. James Rachels, *Created from Animals,* p. 209. I write "in the consequentialist field" since, after much hesitation, due in particular to a reflection on the problem of merit, James Rachels recently defined himself as a utilitarian. See his *Can Ethics Provide Answers?* (Lanham: Rowman & Littlefield, 1997), p. 9.

47. Tom Regan, *The Case for Animal Rights,* pp. 324–325.

48. The egalitarian thesis about lives is advanced most notably by Edward Johnson in "Life, Death and Animals," in *Ethics and Animals,* ed. Harlan B. Miller and William H. Williams. Johnson's account is sometimes equated with the view put forward by Steve Sapontzis, but, I think, wrongly so, as what Sapontzis is concerned with is not a comparison among the possible different values of individual lives but rather a comparison between forms of life, within the context of his criticism of human chauvinism. See Steve F. Sapontzis, *Morals, Reason, and Animals,* pp. 216–222.

49. Evelyn Pluhar, *Beyond Prejudice,* pp. 292–295.

50. On the role of contingencies in ethics, and in particular on the relationship between morality and modality, see among others the enlightening essay by Colin McGinn, "Apes, Humans, Aliens, Vampires and Robots," in *The Great Ape Project. Equality beyond Humanity,* ed. Paola Cavalieri and Peter Singer (New York: St. Martin's Press, 1994).

51. See David DeGrazia, "Great Apes, Dolphins, and the concept of Personhood," *Southern Journal of Philosophy,* vol. 35 (1997). The collection of readings is Paola Cavalieri and Peter Singer, ed., *The Great Ape Project.*

52. Daniel C. Dennett, "Conditions of Personhood," in *The Identities of Persons,* ed. Amélie O. Rorty (Berkeley: University of California Press, 1976).

53. See Paola Cavalieri and Peter Singer, eds., *The Great Ape Project,* in particular sect. 2 and sect. 5. For more data on self-consciousness see among others Sue Savage-Rumbaugh and Roger Lewin, *Kanzi. The Ape at the Brink of the Human Mind* (London: Doubleday, 1994); Sue Taylor Parker, Robert W. Mitchell, and Maria L. Boccia, eds., *Self-awareness in Animals and Humans. Developmental Perspectives* (Cambridge: Cambridge University Press, 1994); and Frans de Waal, *Good Natured. The Origins of Right and Wrong in Humans and Other Animals* (Cambridge, Mass.: Harvard University Press, 1996).

54. David DeGrazia, "Great Apes, Dolphins, and the Concept of Personhood," p. 316.

55. Ibid., p. 315.

56. Hugo Adam Bedau, "International Human Rights," in *And Justice for All*, ed. Tom Regan and Donald VanDeVeer (Totowa, N.J.: Rowman & Allanheld, 1983), p. 290.

57. David DeGrazia, "Great Apes, Dolphins, and the Concept of Personhood," p. 308.

58. Ibid., p. 301.

59. On the essential characteristics of the concept of person, see A. Trendelenburg's fundamental study, "A Contribution to the History of the Word Person," *The Monist*, vol. 20 (1910). For a more detailed presentation of the view I advance, cf. Paola Cavalieri and Peter Singer, "The Great Ape Project," in *Ape, Man, Apeman: Changing Views since 1600*, ed. Raymond Corbey and Bert Theunissen (Leiden: Leiden University Press, 1995).

60. On the subject of the ambiguity of the Stoics and of the relation between the notion of person and that ability to own oneself which excludes being another's property, cf. William O. Stephens, "Masks, Androids, and Primates: The Evolution of the Concept 'Person,' " *Etica & Animali*, vol. 9 (1998): 117–118. For Leonard Nelson, see *A System of Ethics*, trans. N. Guterman (New Haven: Yale University Press, 1956), p. 9, and for Steve F. Sapontzis, see "Aping Persons—Pro and Con," in *The Great Ape Project*, ed. Paola Cavalieri and Peter Singer. As for P. F. Strawson, see the short mention in *Individuals* (London: Methuen, 1959), p. 104.

61. John Locke, *An Essay Concerning Human Understanding* (Cleveland: World Publishing Co., 1964), book 2, chap. 9, part 29, p. 211.

62. Immanuel Kant, *Anthropology from a Pragmatic Point of View*, trans. Victor Lyle Dowdell (Carbondale, Ill.: Southern Illinois University Press, 1978), book 1, part 1.

63. See for example the way H. Lyn White Miles utilizes the notion in "Language and the Ourang-utan: The Old 'Person' of the Forest," in *The Great Ape Project*, ed. Paola Cavalieri and Peter Singer, p. 53.

64. On the distinction between the descriptive and the normative sense of the concept of person, see among others Joel Feinberg, "Abortion," in *Matters of Life and Death*, ed. Tom Regan, 2d ed. (New York: Random House, 1986); see also Dieter Birnbacher, "The Great Apes—Why They Have a Right to Life," *Etica & Animali*, vol. 8 (1996): 142–144. For the definition of person quoted see Michael Tooley, *Abortion and Infanticide*, p. 87.

65. Daniel C. Dennett, "Conditions of Personhood," p. 193.

66. Harlan B. Miller, "What's the Point of Personhood?" typescript, April 1997.

67. The connection between personhood and possession of self-consciousness in the specific sense is frequent. An example is provided by John Harris who, in a passage focusing on how to recognize persons, directly recasts the question in terms of how to identify the presence of self-consciousness. See John Harris, *The Value of Life* (London: Routledge, 1985), p.19. Also see the

more recent "The Concept of the Person and the Value of Life," *Kennedy Institute of Ethics Journal,* vol. 9 (1999).

68. A somewhat similar conclusion is reached by Tom L. Beauchamp who, though starting from a different analysis, suggests that we "erase [the concept of person] from normative analysis, and replace it with more specific concepts and relevant properties." See "The Failures of Theories of Personhood," *Kennedy Institute of Ethics Journal,* vol. 9 (1999): 319.

Chapter 6

1. Cf. in general note 7 of Chap. 2. For Mackie see also pp. 134–136 of his *Ethics. Inventing Right and Wrong* (London: Penguin, 1990). For Strawson see "Social Morality and Individual Ideal," *Philosophy,* vol. 136 (1961).

2. John Stuart Mill, "On Liberty," in J. S. Mill, *On Liberty and Other Essays* (Oxford: Oxford University Press, 1998), p. 14.

3. Josef Raz, "Right-based Moralities," in *Theories of Rights,* ed. Jeremy Waldron (Oxford: Oxford University Press, 1984), p. 198.

4. D. D. Raphael qualifies the traditional idea that social and economic (or positive) rights are a recent addition to the theory by observing that some of them, and in particular the right to education, were already present in various authors of the eighteenth century, from Thomas Paine to Babeuf. And yet he remarks that such rights rather than as "human rights" are to be classified as "citizen's rights." Cf. D. D. Raphael, "Human Rights, Old and New," in *Political Theory and the Rights of Man,* ed. D. D. Raphael (London: Macmillan, 1967).

5. Onora O'Neill, "Do We Need Environmental Values?" typescript, May 1996.

6. Brenda Almond, "Rights," in *A Companion to Ethics,* ed. Peter Singer (Oxford: Blackwell, 1991), p. 263.

7. Jeremy Bentham, "Anarchical Fallacies," in *Human Rights,* ed. A. I. Melden (Belmont: Wadsworth, 1970), pp. 28, 32.

8. Margaret MacDonald, "Natural Rights," in *Theories of Rights,* ed. J. Waldron, p. 32. The essay originally appeared in *Proceedings of the Aristotelian Society 1947–48,* The Aristotelian Society, 1949.

9. An echo of this meaning can still be found in Rawls, where he defines as "natural" the duties that apply to individuals without regard to their voluntary acts and irrespective of their institutional relationships. See John Rawls, *A Theory of Justice* (Oxford: Oxford University Press, 1973), pp. 114–117.

10. It is Article 4: "No one shall be held in slavery or servitude; slavery and the slave trade shall be prohibited in all their forms."

11. Cf. John Rawls, *The Law of Peoples* (Cambridge, Mass.: Harvard University Press, 1999), pp. 26–27. On the changes that the very concept of the sovereignty of the nation-state has undergone owing to the notion of human

rights, see also Robert E. Goodin, Carole Pateman, and Roy Pateman, "Simian Sovereignty," *Political Theory,* vol. 25 (1997): 821–849.

12. Catharine A. MacKinnon, "Crimes of War, Crimes of Peace," in *On Human Rights,* ed. Stephen Shute and Susan Hurley (New York: Basic Books, 1993), p. 95.

13. Thomas Pogge, "How Should Human Rights Be Conceived?" *Jahrbuch für Recht und Ethik,* vol. 3 (1995).

14. Ibid., p. 114. One can perceive here the echo of a view that already in the 1960s had been defended by Bernard Mayo: "Human rights . . . are claimed of political authorities. . . . [A] human right is a claim to *action* (or inaction) *by a State government.* . . ." See B. Mayo, "What are Human Rights?" in *Political Theory and the Rights of Man,* ed. D. D. Raphael, pp. 73 and 77.

15. Cf. Joel Feinberg, *Social Philosophy* (Englewood Cliffs, N.J.: Prentice-Hall, 1973), p. 85.

16. Cf. Article I. Concomitantly with the elaboration of the Declaration, UNESCO organized a philosophical meeting on the topic. Such meeting, however, confined itself to gathering influential opinions, without endeavoring to issue a unitary theoretical foundation. This because there was the conviction that the only practicable way could be that of an agreement reached "not on the basis of common speculative ideas, but on common practical ideas, not on the affirmation of one and the same conception . . . but upon the affirmation of a single body of beliefs for guidance in action." Cf. Jacques Maritain, "Introduction," in UNESCO, *Human Rights: Comments and Interpretations: A Symposium* (London & New York: Allan Wingate, 1949), p. 10. Maritain also relates the emblematic statement of one of the participants to the meeting: "We agree about the rights but *on condition that no one asks us why*"—a statement that contributes well to explain the conciseness of Article I (ibid., p. 9).

17. Hugo Adam Bedau, "International Human Rights," in *And Justice for All,* ed. Tom Regan and Donald VanDeVeer (Totowa, N.J.: Rowman & Allanheld, 1983), p. 298.

18. A. I. Melden, *Rights and Persons* (Berkeley: University of California Press, 1977), p. 200. When, in fact, in an article dating back to the fifties of the past century he had actually endeavored to find "a basis for human rights," and had identified it in moral agency, Melden was obliged to attribute "lunatics" and "criminally insane" less-than-equal rights. See "Symposium: The Concept of Universal Human Rights—I. A. I. Melden," in American Philosophical Association, *Science, Language, and Human Rights* (Philadelphia: University of Pennsylvania Press, 1952), vol. 1, pp. 186–187.

19. Gregory Vlastos, "Justice and Equality," in *Theories of Rights,* ed. J. Waldron. The essay originally appeared in *Social Justice,* ed. Richard B. Brandt (Englewood Cliffs, N.J.: Prentice-Hall, 1962).

20. Ibid., p. 56. It is easy to notice here an analogy with the argument in defense of subjectivity as an inclusive criterion of moral status.

21. Ibid., p. 57.

22. Ibid., p. 58. Vlastos writes "instrumental" instead of "extrinic," but in this context the use of this adjective might create confusion.

23. Ibid.

24. Richard Wasserstrom, "Rights, Human Rights, and Racial Discrimination," in *Moral Problems*, ed. James Rachels, 3d ed. (New York: Harper & Row, 1979).

25. Ibid., p. 17.

26. Ibid., p. 19.

27. Ibid., pp. 11–12, 19.

28. Alan Gewirth, *Reason and Morality* (Chicago: The University of Chicago Press, 1978). See also his *Human Rights* (Chicago: The University of Chicago Press, 1982).

29. After observing that the criteria that assert rights should not necessarily be moral or legal but can be of a different sort—for example, logical or intellectual—Gewirth explains such claims in the following terms: "The criteria on which [the agent] grounds these 'rights' . . . are not moral but rather prudential . . . What grounds his [*sic*] judgment is his own agency-needs, not those of the persons about whom he makes the judgment." Alan Gewirth, *Reason and Morality*, pp. 71 ff.

30. On the criterion of relevant similarities see ibid., pp. 104 ff. The level of the requisite of intentionality is determined by the inclusion among the beings relevantly similar to the reflective agent of newborn infants and of the individuals with mental disabilities ("mentally deficient persons"): cf. ibid., pp. 141–142. But see also below, note 35.

31. For the transition from the prudential to the moral, see ibid., p.146; for the *Principle of Generic Consistency* or PGC, cf. ibid., p. 135. A summary of the argument can be found in Alan Gewirth, "The Basis and Content of Human Rights," in *Nomos XXIII: Human Rights*, ed. J. Roland Pennock and John W. Chapman (New York: New York University Press, 1981).

32. Alan Gewirth, *Reason and Morality*, pp. 144, 189, 197–198.

33. Richard Hare, *Freedom and Reason* (Oxford: Clarendon Press, 1990), chap. 8.

34. Cf. Daniel C. Dennett, "Animal Consciousness: What Matters and Why," *Social Research*, vol. 62 (1995): 702. For his part, Dennett includes in this category, in addition to members of other species, also "human beings when they are newborn."

35. For a synthesis of the argument see for example David DeGrazia, *Taking Animals Seriously. Mental Life and Moral Status* (Cambridge: Cambridge University Press, 1996), chap. 6 and pp. 166–172.

36. Cf. Richard Dawkins, "Gaps in the Mind," in *The Great Ape Project*.

Equality beyond Humanity, ed. Paola Cavalieri and Peter Singer (New York: St. Martin's Press, 1994).

37. Apart, of course, from instances of paternalism: cf. for example Alan Gewirth, *Reason and Morality,* pp. 141–142.

38. On this subject see among other things the debate on the "discrimination against the disabled" summarized in Peter Singer and Helga Kuhse, "The Future of Baby Doe," *The New York Review of Books,* 1 Mar. 1984, and the events related by Peter Singer in "On Being Silenced in Germany," *The New York Review of Books,* 15 Aug. 1991.

39. Gary L. Francione, *Animals, Property and the Law* (Philadelphia: Temple University Press, 1995), p. 10.

40. Catharine A. MacKinnon, "Crimes of War, Crimes of Peace," in *On Human Rights,* ed. Stephen Shute and Susan Hurley, p. 103.

41. The notion of *egalitarian plateau* is Ronald Dworkin's. For an analysis of its role in the contemporary debate, see Will Kymlicka, *Contemporary Political Philosophy. An Introduction* (Oxford: Clarendon Press, 1990), p. 5.

42. Aristotle, *Politics,* I, 2, 1253 b.

43. Only if, and when, the decisive step of the abolition of any sort of official discrimination has included nonhuman animals among the beneficiaries of the protection the expanded theory affords, it will become possible to deal with the problem of specific transactions between individual rightholders, and with the ways of settling unavoidable conflicts of interests. For though a commitment to the rights envisaged by the expanded theory does not coincide with an interactional commitment, it is not entirely separate from such an idea, because the claim that societies ought to be organized so that the individuals living in them should not endure discriminatory or degrading treatment is naturally connected with a more inclusive concern for the protection of individuals. A seminal attempt at immediately coupling the two commitments can however be found in Paola Cavalieri and Peter Singer, eds., *The Great Ape Project.*

44. For this statement, as well as for the following one, cf. Thomas Pogge, "How Should Human Rights Be Conceived?" p. 116 and p. 109. Such analysis seems to disprove the distinction between individual morality and political morality which has been drawn, with variations, by Jean-Yves Goffi in *Le philosophe et ses animaux. Du statut éthique de l'animal* (Nîmes: Éditions Jaqueline Chambon, 1994), and by Ursula Wolf in *Das Tier in der Moral* (Frankfurt: Vittorio Klostermann, 1990).

Bibliography

Allen, Colin, and Marc Bekoff. *Species of Mind: The Philosophy and Biology of Cognitive Ethology.* Cambridge (Mass.): MIT Press, 1997.

Almond, Brenda. "Rights." In *A Companion to Ethics,* ed. Peter Singer. Oxford: Blackwell, 1991.

Aquinas, Thomas. *Summa contra Gentiles,* trans. English Dominican Fathers. New York: Benzinger Brothers, 1928.

Aristotle. *Nicomachean Ethics,* trans. W. D. Ross. Oxford: Oxford University Press, 1980.

———. *Politics,* trans. H. Rackham. Cambridge (Mass.): Harvard University Press, 1950.

Barry, Brian. *Theories of Justice.* Berkeley: University of California Press, 1989.

Beauchamp, Tom L. "The Failures of Theories of Personhood." *Kennedy Institute of Ethics Journal* 9 (1999): 309–324.

Bedau, Hugo Adam. "International Human Rights." In *And Justice for All,* ed. T. Regan and D. VanDeVeer. Totowa (N.J.): Rowman & Allanheld, 1983.

Bekoff, Marc. "Cognitive Ethology: The Comparative Study of Animal Minds." In *Blackwell Companion to Cognitive Science,* ed. W. Bechtel and G. Graham. Oxford: Blackwell, 1998.

Bekoff, Marc, and Colin Allen. "Cognitive Ethology: Slayers, Skeptics, and Proponents." In *Anthropomorphism, Anecdotes, and Animals,* ed. Robert W. Mitchell, Nicholas S. Thompson, and H. Lyn White Miles. Albany: State University of New York Press, 1997.

Bekoff, Marc, and Colin Allen. "Intentional Communication and Social Play: How and Why Animals Negotiate and Agree to Play." In *Animal Play: Evolutionary, Comparative, and Ecological Perspectives,* ed. Marc Bekoff and J. A. Byers. Cambridge: Cambridge University Press, 1998.

Benn, Stanley. "Egalitarianism and Equal Consideration of Interests." In *Nomos IX: Equality,* ed. J. R. Pennock and J. W. Chapman. New York: Atherton Press, 1967.

Bentham, Jeremy. *An Introduction to the Principles of Morals and Legislation.* New York: Hafner Press, 1948.

———. "Anarchical Fallacies." In *Human Rights,* ed. A. I. Melden. Belmont: Wadsworth, 1970.

Birnbacher, Dieter. "The Great Apes—Why They Have a Right to Life." *Etica & Animali* 8 (1996): 142–154.

Callicott, J. Baird. "Animal Liberation: A Triangular Affair." *Environmental Ethics* 2 (1980): 311–338.

———. "Hume's *Is/Ought* Dichotomy and the Relation of Ecology to Leopold's Land Ethic." *Environmental Ethics* 4 (1982): 163–174.

———. "Intrinsic Value in Nature: A Metaethical Analysis," *Electronic Journal of Analytic Philosophy* 3 (1995). (http://www.phil.indiana.edu/ejap/1995.spring/callicott.abs.html)

Carruthers, Peter. "Brute Experience." *Journal of Philosophy* 86 (1989): 258–269.

———. *The Animals Issue.* Cambridge: Cambridge University Press, 1992.

———. "Natural Theories of Consciousness." *European Journal of Philosophy* 2 (1998): 203–222.

Cavalieri, Paola. "L'humanité au-delà des humains." *Le Débat* 108 (2000): 184–192.

Cavalieri, Paola, and Harlan B. Miller. "Automata, Receptacles and Selves." *Psyche* 5 (1999). (http://psyche.cs.monash.edu.au/v5/psyche-5-04-cavalieri.html)

Cavalieri, Paola, and Peter Singer, eds. *The Great Ape Project. Equality beyond Humanity.* New York: St. Martin's Press, 1994.

———. "The Great Ape Project." In *Ape, Man, Apeman: Changing Views since 1600,* ed. R. Corbey and B. Theunissen. Leiden: Leiden University Press, 1995.

Cavalieri, Paola, and Will Kymlicka. "Expanding the Social Contract." *Etica & Animali* 8 (1996): 5–33.

Cohen, Carl. "The Case for the Use of Animals in Biomedical Research." *New England Journal of Medicine* 315 (1986): 865–870.

Cribb, Julian. "Now it's Homo Gorillas." *The Australian,* 3 May 1996.

Darwin, Charles. "The Descent of Man." In Charles Darwin, *The Origin of Species and The Descent of Man.* New York: Random House, n.d.

Davis, David B. *The Problem of Slavery in Western Culture.* Ithaca: Cornell University Press, 1969.

Dawkins, Richard. "Gaps in the Mind." In *The Great Ape Project. Equality beyond Humanity,* ed. Paola Cavalieri and Peter Singer. New York: St. Martin's Press, 1994.

DeGrazia, David. "The Distinction between Equality in Moral Status and Deserving Equal Consideration." *Between the Species* 7 (1991): 73–77.

———. *Taking Animals Seriously. Mental Life and Moral Status.* Cambridge: Cambridge University Press, 1996.

———. "Great Apes, Dolphins, and the Concept of Personhood." *Southern Journal of Philosophy* 35 (1997): 301–320.

Dennett, Daniel C. "Conditions of Personhood." In *The Identities of Persons,* ed. A. O. Rorty. Berkeley: University of California Press, 1976.

———. "Animal Consciousness: What Matters and Why." *Social Research* 62 (1995): 691–710.

Descartes, René. "Discourse on the Method." In René Descartes, *Discourse on the Method and Meditations on First Philosophy,* ed. David Weissman. New Haven & London: Yale University Press, 1996.

De Waal, Frans. *Good Natured. The Origins of Right and Wrong in Humans and Other Animals.* Cambridge (Mass.): Harvard University Press, 1996.

Diamond, Jared. "The Third Chimpanzee." In *The Great Ape Project. Equality beyond Humanity,* ed. Paola Cavalieri and Peter Singer. New York: St. Martin's Press, 1994.

Dombrowski, Daniel A. *Babies and Beasts. The Argument from Marginal Cases.* Chicago: University of Illinois Press, 1997.

Dworkin, Gerald, R. G. Frey, and Sissela Bok. *Euthanasia and Physician-Assisted Suicide.* Cambridge: Cambridge University Press, 1998.

Dworkin, Ronald. *Taking Rights Seriously.* Cambridge (Mass.): Harvard University Press, 1979.

Feinberg, Joel. *Social Philosophy.* Englewood Cliffs (N.J.): Prentice-Hall, 1973.

———. *Rights, Justice and the Bounds of Liberty.* Princeton: Princeton University Press, 1980.

———. "Abortion." In *Matters of Life and Death,* ed. T. Regan. 2d ed. New York: Random House, 1986.

Fletcher, Joseph. *Humanhood: Essays in Biomedical Ethics.* New York: Prometheus Books, 1980.

Foppa, Carlo. "L'ontologie de Hans Jonas à la lumière de la théorie de l'évolution." In *Nature et descendance. Hans Jonas et le principe "Responsabilité,"* ed. D. Müller and R. Simon. Lausanne: Labor et Fides, 1993.

———. "L'insoutenable poids de la théorie de l'évolution." *Etica & Animali* 8 (1996): 96–114.

Frankena, William K. "The Concept of Morality." *Journal of Philosophy* 63 (1966): 688–696.

———. "Ethics and the Environment." In *Ethics and Problems of the 21st Century,* ed. K. E. Goodpaster and K. M. Sayre. Notre Dame: University of Notre Dame Press, 1979.

Francione, Gary L. *Animals, Property, and the Law.* Philadelphia: Temple University Press, 1995.

Frey, Raymond G. *Interests and Rights: The Case Against Animals.* Oxford: Clarendon Press, 1980.

———. "Animal Parts, Human Wholes." In *Biomedical Ethics Reviews,* ed. J. M. Humber and R. F. Almeder. Clifton (N.J.): Humana Press, 1987.

———. "Autonomy and the Value of Animal Life." *The Monist* 70 (1987): 50–63.

Gauthier, David. *Morals by Agreement.* Oxford: Clarendon Press, 1986.

———. "Intervista," ed. Lorenzo Sacconi, *Notizie di Politeia* 4 (1988): 16–23.

Gewirth, Alan. *Reason and Morality.* Chicago: The University of Chicago Press, 1978.

———. "The Basis and Content of Human Rights." In *Nomos XXIII: Human Rights,* ed. J. R. Pennock and J. W. Chapman. New York: New York University Press, 1981.

———. *Human Rights.* Chicago: The University of Chicago Press, 1982.

Godlovitch, Stanley, Roslind Godlovitch, and John Harris, eds. *Animals, Men and Morals.* New York: Grove Press, 1972.

Goffi, Jean-Yves. *Le philosophe et ses animaux. Du statut éthique de l'animal.* Nîmes: Éditions Jacqueline Chambon, 1994.

Gómez, Juan Carlos. "Are Apes Persons? The Case for Primate Intersubjectivity." *Etica & Animali* 9 (1998): 51–63.

Goodall, Jane. *The Chimpanzees of Gombe.* Cambridge: Cambridge University Press, 1989.

Goodin, Robert E., Carole Pateman, and Roy Pateman. "Simian Sovereignty." *Political Theory* 25 (1997): 821–849.

Goodpaster, Kenneth E. "From Egoism to Environmentalism." In *Ethics and Problems of the 21st Century,* ed. K. E. Goodpaster and K. M. Sayre. Notre Dame: University of Notre Dame Press, 1979.

Griffin, Donald R. *The Question of Animal Awareness.* New York: The Rockefeller University Press, 1976.

———. *Animal Thinking.* Cambridge (Mass.): Harvard University Press, 1984.

———. *Animal Minds.* Chicago: The University of Chicago Press, 1992.

Haraway, Donna. *Primate Visions. Gender, Race, and Nature in the World of Modern Science.* London: Routledge, 1989.

Hare, Richard. "Rules of War and Moral Reasoning." *Philosophy & Public Affairs* 1 (1972): 166–181.

———. *Freedom and Reason.* Oxford: Clarendon Press, 1990.

Harris, John. *The Value of Life.* London: Routledge, 1985.

———. "The Concept of the Person and the Value of Life." *Kennedy Institute of Ethics Journal* 9 (1999): 293–308.

Herman, Louis M., Adam A. Pack, and Palmer Morrel-Samuels. "Representational and Conceptual Skills of Dolphins." In *Language and Communi-*

cation: Comparative Perspectives, ed. H. L. Roitblat, L. M. Herman, and P. E. Nachtigall. Hillsdale (N.J.): Lawrence Erlbaum Associates, 1993.

Herman, Louis M., Adam A. Pack, and Amy M. Wood. "Bottlenose Dolphins Can Generalize Rules and Develop Abstract Concepts." *Marine Mammal Science* 10 (1994): 70–79.

Herzing, Denise L., and Thomas I. White. "Dolphins and the Question of Personhood." *Etica & Animali* 9 (1998): 64–84.

Hoff, Christina. *The Moral Domain: An Inquiry into Its Extent and Limits.* Ph.D. diss., Brandeis University, May 1979 (University Microfilms International. Ann Arbor, Mich.).

Hume, David. *A Treatise of Human Nature.* Oxford: Oxford University Press, 1888.

Jamieson, Dale. "Method and Moral Theory." In *A Companion to Ethics,* ed. Peter Singer. Oxford: Blackwell, 1991.

Johnson, Edward. *Species and Morality.* Ph.D. diss., Princeton University, July 1976 (University Microfilms International. Ann Arbor, Mich.).

———. "Life, Death, and Animals." In *Ethics and Animals,* ed. Harlan B. Miller and W. H. Williams. Clifton (N.J.): Humana Press, 1983.

———. "Treating the Dirt: Environmental Ethics and Moral Theory." In *Earthbound,* ed. Tom Regan. Philadelphia: Temple University Press, 1984.

Jonas, Hans. *The Phenomenon of Life.* Chicago: The University of Chicago Press, 1966.

Kant, Immanuel. *Foundations of the Metaphysics of Morals,* trans. Lewis W. Beck. Upper Saddle River (N.J.): Prentice-Hall, 1997.

———. *Lectures on Ethics,* trans. Louis Infield. New York: Harper and Row, 1963.

———. *Anthropology from a Pragmatic Point of View,* trans. Victor Lyle Dowdell. Carbondale (Ill.): Southern Illinois University Press, 1978.

———. *The Philosophy of Law,* trans. W. Hastie. Edinburgh: T. & T. Clark, 1887.

Kuhse, Helga. *The Sanctity-of-Life Doctrine in Medicine: A Critique.* Oxford: Clarendon Press, 1987.

Kymlicka, Will. *Contemporary Political Philosophy. An Introduction.* Oxford: Clarendon Press, 1990.

Leopold, Aldo. *A Sand County Almanac.* Oxford: Oxford University Press, 1949.

Linden, Eugene. "Can Animals Think?" *Time,* 29 Mar. 1993.

Locke, John. *An Essay Concerning Human Understanding.* Cleveland: World Publishing Co., 1964.

Lyons, David. "Utility and Rights." In *Theories of Rights,* ed. J. Waldron. Oxford: Oxford University Press, 1984.

MacDonald, Margaret. "Natural Rights." In *Theories of Rights,* ed. J. Waldron. Oxford: Oxford University Press, 1984.

MacIntyre, Alasdair C. "Hume on 'Is' and 'Ought.' " In *The Is-Ought Question,* ed. W. D. Hudson. London: Macmillan, 1969.

———. *After Virtue.* Notre Dame: University of Notre Dame Press, 1984.

Mackie, J. L. *Ethics. Inventing Right and Wrong.* Harmondsworth: Penguin Books, 1990.

MacKinnon, Katharine A. "Crimes of War, Crimes of Peace." In *On Human Rights,* ed. S. Shute and S. Hurley. New York: Basic Books, 1993.

Mayo, Bernard. "What are Human Rights?" In *Political Theory and the Rights of Man,* ed. D. D. Raphael. London: Macmillan, 1967.

McGinn, Colin. "Apes, Humans, Aliens, Vampires and Robots." In *The Great Ape Project. Equality beyond Humanity,* ed. Paola Cavalieri and Peter Singer. New York: St. Martin's Press, 1994.

———. "Animal Minds, Animal Morality." *Social Research* 62 (1995): 731–747.

Melden, A. I. "Symposium: The Concept of Universal Human Rights—I: A. I. Melden." In *Science, Language, and Human Rights,* vol. 1. American Philosophical Association. Philadelphia: University of Pennsylvania Press, 1952.

———. *Rights and Persons.* Berkeley: University of California Press, 1977.

Midgley, Mary. "The Absence of a Gap between Facts and Values." *Aristotelian Society Supplementary* 54 (1980): 207–223.

———. *Animals and Why They Matter.* Athens: The University of Georgia Press, 1983.

Miles, H. Lyn White. "Language and the Ourang-utan: The Old 'Person' of the Forest." In *The Great Ape Project. Equality beyond Humanity,* ed. Paola Cavalieri and Peter Singer. New York: St. Martin's Press, 1994.

Mill, John Stuart. "On Liberty." In John Stuart Mill, *On Liberty and Other Essays.* Oxford: Oxford University Press, 1998.

———. "Utilitarianism." In John Stuart Mill, *On Liberty and Other Essays.* Oxford: Oxford University Press, 1998.

Miller, Harlan B. "On Abortion." 1993. (http://server.phil.vt.edu/Miller/papers/abortion.html)

———. "Science, Ethics, and Moral Status." *Between the Species* 10 (1994): 10–18.

———. "What's the Point of Personhood?" Typescript, April 1997.

Mitchell, Robert W. "Humans, Nonhumans and Personhood." In *The Great Ape Project. Equality beyond Humanity,* ed. Paola Cavalieri and Peter Singer. New York: St. Martin's Press, 1994.

Moore, G. E. *Principia Ethica.* Cambridge: Cambridge University Press, 1993.

Morgan, David. "Scientists: Apes Have Strong Communication Skills." Reuters, *News America Digital Publishing,* 15 Feb. 1998.

Nagel, Thomas. *The Possibility of Altruism.* Oxford: Clarendon Press, 1970.

———. "What Is It Like to Be a Bat?" *Philosophical Review* 83 (1974): 435–450.

————. "Ethics as an Autonomous Theoretical Subject." In *Morality as a Biological Phenomenon,* ed. G. S. Stent. Berkeley: University of California Press, 1978.

Nelson, Leonard. *A System of Ethics,* trans. N. Guterman. New Haven: Yale University Press, 1956.

Norton, David Fate. "Hume, Atheism, and the Autonomy of Morals." In *Hume's Philosophy of Religion,* ed. M. Hester. Winston Salem: Wake Forest University Press, 1986.

Noske, Barbara. "Great Apes as Anthropological Subjects—Deconstructing Anthropocentrism." In *The Great Ape Project. Equality beyond Humanity,* ed. Paola Cavalieri and Peter Singer. New York: St. Martin's Press, 1994.

Nozick, Robert. *Anarchy, State and Utopia.* New York: Basic Books, 1974.

————. "About Mammals and People." *The New York Times Book Review,* 27 Nov. 1983.

O'Neill, Onora. "Kantian Ethics." In *A Companion to Ethics,* ed. Peter Singer. Oxford: Blackwell, 1991.

————. "Do We Need Environmental Values?" Typescript, May 1996.

Parfit, Derek. *Reasons and Persons.* Oxford: Oxford University Press, 1986.

Pepperberg, Irene M. "A Communicative Approach to Animal Cognition: A Study of Conceptual Abilities of an African Grey Parrot." In *Cognitive Ethology: The Minds of Other Animals,* ed. C. A. Ristau. Hillsdale (N.J.): Lawrence Erlbaum Associates, 1991.

Pluhar, Evelyn. "Speciesism: A Form of Bigotry or a Justified View?" *Between the Species* 4 (1988): 83–96.

————. *Beyond Prejudice. The Moral Significance of Human and Nonhuman Animals.* Durham: Duke University Press, 1995.

Pogge, Thomas. "How Should Human Rights Be Conceived?" *Jahrbuch für Recht und Ethik* 3 (1995): 103–120.

Poole, Joyce H. "An Exploration of a Commonality between Ourselves and Elephants." *Etica & Animali* 9 (1998): 85–110.

Porphyry. *De abstinentia.* Paris: Les Belles Lettres, 1977.

Pybus, Elisabeth M., and Alexander Broadie. "Kant on the Maltreatment of Animals." *Philosophy* 53 (1978): 560–561.

Rachels, James. "Do Animals Have a Right to Life?" In *Ethics and Animals,* ed. Harlan B. Miller and W. H. Williams. Clifton (N.J.): Humana Press, 1983.

————. *The End of Life. Euthanasia and Morality.* Oxford: Oxford University Press, 1986.

————. *Created from Animals. The Moral Implications of Darwinism.* Oxford: Oxford University Press, 1990.

————. *Can Ethics Provide Answers?* Lanham: Rowman & Littlefield, 1997.

Raphael, D. D. "Human Rights, Old and New." In *Political Theory and the Rights of Man,* ed. D. D. Raphael. London: Macmillan, 1967.

Rawls, John. *A Theory of Justice.* Oxford: Oxford University Press, 1973.

———. *The Law of Peoples.* Cambridge (Mass.): Harvard University Press, 1999.

Raz, Joseph. "Right-Based Moralities." In *Theories of Rights,* ed. J. Waldron. Oxford: Oxford University Press, 1984.

Regan, Tom. *All that Dwell Therein.* Berkeley: University of California Press, 1982.

———. *The Case for Animal Rights.* Berkeley: University of California Press, 1983.

———. "Animal Rights." In *Encyclopedia of Animal Rights and Animal Welfare,* ed. Marc Bekoff with Carron A. Meaney. Westport (Conn.): Greenwood Press, 1998.

Regan, Tom, and Peter Singer, eds. *Animal Rights and Human Obligations.* Englewood Cliffs (N.J.): Prentice-Hall, 1976.

Richards, David. *A Theory of Reasons for Action.* Oxford: Clarendon Press, 1971.

Rollin, Bernard. *The Unheeded Cry: Animal Consciousness, Animal Pain, and Science.* Oxford: Oxford University Press, 1989.

Rorty, Richard. "Human Rights, Rationality and Sentimentality." In *On Human Rights,* ed. S. Shute and S. Hurley. New York: Basic Books, 1993.

Ross, W. D. *The Right and the Good.* Indianapolis: Hackett Publishing Company, 1988.

Sagan, Carl and Ann Druyan. *Shadows of Forgotten Ancestors.* New York: Random House, 1992.

Salt, Henry S. *Animals' Rights.* London: Centaur Press, 1980.

Sapontzis, Steve F. *Morals, Reason and Animals.* Philadelphia: Temple University Press, 1987.

———. "Everyday Morality and Animal Rights." *Between the Species* 3 (1987): 107–118.

———. "Autonomy as an Excuse for All-Too-Human Chauvinism." *Between the Species* 8 (1992): 30–33.

———. "Aping Persons—Pro and Con." In *The Great Ape Project. Equality beyond Humanity,* ed. Paola Cavalieri and Peter Singer. New York: St. Martin's Press, 1994.

———. "On Exploiting Inferiors." *Between the Species* 11 (1995): 1–20.

Savage-Rumbaugh, Sue, and Roger Lewin. *Kanzi. The Ape at the Brink of the Human Mind.* London: Doubleday, 1994.

Scanlon, Thomas. *What We Owe to Each Other.* Cambridge (Mass.): Harvard University Press, 1998.

Schneewind, J. B. *Sidgwick's Ethics and Victorian Moral Philosophy.* Oxford: Clarendon Press, 1977.

Schopenhauer, Arthur. *On the Basis of Morality,* trans. E. F. J. Payne. Indianapolis: Bobbs-Merrill, 1965.

Schweitzer, Albert. *Civilization and Ethics.* 3d ed. London: A. C. Black, 1949.

Searle, John R. "Animal Minds." *Etica & Animali* 9 (1998): 37–50.

Sheets-Johnstone, Maxine. "Taking Evolution Seriously: A Matter of Primate Intelligence." *Etica & Animali* 8 (1996): 115–130.

———. "Consciousness: A Natural History." *Journal of Consciousness Studies* 5 (1998): 260–294.

Sidgwick, Henry. *The Methods of Ethics*. 7th ed. (1907). Indianapolis: Hackett Publishing Company, 1981.

Singer, Peter. "Sidgwick and Reflective Equilibrium." *The Monist* 58 (1974): 490–517.

———. *Practical Ethics*. Cambridge: Cambridge University Press, 1979.

———. *Animal Liberation*. 2d ed. New York: The New York Review of Books, 1990.

———. "On Being Silenced in Germany." *The New York Review of Books*, 15 Aug. 1991.

———. *Rethinking Life and Death. The Collapse of Our Traditional Ethics*. Oxford: Oxford University Press, 1995.

Singer, Peter, and Helga Kuhse. "The Future of Baby Doe." *The New York Review of Books*, 1 Mar. 1984.

Sommer, Volker. " 'Sind Affen denn auch Leute?' Ja. Denn zwischen Natur und Kultur fließen die Übergänge." *Etica & Animali* 8 (1996): 75–95.

Stephens, William O. "Masks, Androids, and Primates: The Evolution of the Concept 'Person.' " *Etica & Animali* 9 (1998): 111–127.

Strawson, P. F. *Individuals*. London: Methuen, 1959.

———. "Social Morality and Individual Ideal." *Philosophy* 136 (1961): 1–17.

Sumner, L. W. *Abortion and Moral Theory*. Princeton: Princeton University Press, 1981.

Taylor Parker, Sue, Robert W. Mitchell, and Maria L. Boccia, eds. *Self-awareness in Animals and Humans*. Cambridge: Cambridge University Press, 1994.

Taylor, Paul. *Respect for Nature*. Princeton: Princeton University Press, 1986.

Thompson, Judith Jarvis. "A Defense of Abortion." *Philosophy & Public Affairs* 1 (1971): 47–66.

Tooley, Michael. "Abortion and Infanticide." *Philosophy & Public Affairs* 2 (1972): 37–65.

———. *Abortion and Infanticide*. Oxford: Oxford University Press, 1983.

———. "Speciesism and Basic Moral Principles." *Etica & Animali* 9 (1998): 5–36.

Trendelenburg, Adolf. "A Contribution to the History of the Word 'Person.' " *The Monist* 20 (1910): 336–363.

UNESCO. *Human Rights: Comments and Interpretations: A Symposium*. London & New York: Allan Wingate, 1949.

VanDeVeer, Donald. "Whither Baby Doe?" In *Matters of Life and Death,* ed. Tom Regan. 2d ed. New York: Random House, 1986.

Vlastos, Gregory. "Justice and Equality." In *Theories of Rights,* ed. Jeremy Waldron. Oxford: Oxford University Press, 1984.

Warnock, Geoffrey J. *The Object of Morality*. London: Methuen, 1971.

Warnock, Mary. *Ethics since 1900*. 3d ed. Oxford: Oxford University Press, 1990.

Warren, Mary Anne. *Moral Status*. Oxford: Clarendon Press, 1997.

Wasserstrom, Richard. "Rights, Human Rights and Racial Discrimination." In *Moral Problems,* ed. James Rachels. 3d ed. New York: Harper & Row, 1979.

Whiten, Andrew. "Imitation, Pretense, and Mindreading: Secondary Representation in Comparative Primatology and Developmental Psychology?" In *Reaching into Thought. The Minds of the Great Apes,* ed. A. E. Russon, K. A. Bard and S. Taylor Parker. Cambridge: Cambridge University Press, 1996.

Williams, Bernard. "The Idea of Equality." In *Moral Concepts,* ed. Joel Feinberg. Oxford: Oxford University Press, 1970.

———. "A Critique of Utilitarianism." In J. J. C. Smart and B. Williams, *Utilitarianism: For and Against*. Cambridge: Cambridge University Press, 1973.

Wolf, Ursula. *Das Tier in der Moral*. Frankfurt: Vittorio Klostermann, 1990.

Wreen, Michael. "In Defense of Speciesism." *Ethics & Animals* 5 (1984): 47–60.

Index